CFA INSTITUTE INDUSTRY GUIDES
THE ASSET MANAGEMENT INDUSTRY

by Owen Concannon, CFA

ISBN 978-1-942713-03-6
April 2015

ABOUT THE AUTHOR

Owen Concannon, CFA, is a director at Guggenheim Partners, a global investment and advisory firm. He began his career at Financial Research Corporation in Boston, where he was ultimately responsible for overseeing the firm's consulting and investment product research efforts in the exchange-traded fund and alternative investment areas. Subsequently, Mr. Concannon led investment product management and development efforts for Touchstone Investments in Cincinnati. He holds a BA from the College of William and Mary.

CONTENTS

INTRODUCTION

Asset managers serve as a critical link between providers and seekers of investment capital. The asset management industry is an integral component of the global financial services sector, responsible for professionally managing more than $68 trillion in assets owned by a broad range of institutional and individual investors.[1]

Today, thousands of investment managers compete for clients in a highly competitive and mature industry. The universe of firms offering asset management services is varied and ranges from "pure play" independent asset managers to diversified commercial banks, insurance companies, and brokerages—all offering asset management services in addition to complementary and unrelated business lines.

The diversity of asset managers is partially attributable to the multitude of clients the industry serves. Whether these clients are large multinational corporations responsible for multibillion-dollar pension liabilities or individual investors planning for retirement, asset managers play a critical role in achieving the investment objectives that investors require. Increasingly, many asset managers have been aggressively adding investment research and distribution offices overseas to compete on the global stage for the management of client assets.

The asset management industry has naturally evolved alongside an increasingly complex and global capital market landscape as the estimated total global investable capital market size has grown from $64 trillion in 2004 to more than $101.1 trillion as of June 2013 (see **Table 1**).

Asset managers offer a broad range of investment management strategies— informally referred to as "products"—across geographies and capital structures. Although "boutique" asset managers may specialize in specific investment disciplines (e.g., emerging market equities) or methods (e.g., quantitative investing), other "full-service" managers seek to offer an ever-evolving lineup of investment products that cover a breadth of investment styles and asset classes. Increasingly, a "multi-boutique" asset manager structure has emerged whereby a holding company houses a number of affiliated though autonomous boutique asset management firms under one corporate umbrella. This model allows the managers to retain their own unique investment cultures—and often equity ownership stakes—while also drawing on the centralized, shared services of the holding company (e.g., technology, operations, and legal services).

---

[1]Gary Shub, Simon Bartletta, Brent Beardsley, Hélène Donnadieu, Renaud Fages, Craig Hapelt, Benoît Macé, Andy Maguire, and Tjun Tang, "Global Asset Management 2014: Steering the Course to Growth," Boston Consulting Group (16 July 2014): www.bcgperspectives.com/content/articles/financial_institutions_global_asset_management_2014_steering_course_growth.

Table 1. **Global Invested Capital Market by Asset Class**
(as of June 2013, $ trillions)

Asset Class	Market Size	Market Share
Equity		
US equity	$18.20	18%
Non-US equity (developed)	13.85	14
Emerging market equity	3.99	4
Frontier market equity	0.15	0
Alternatives		
Private equity	$2.52	2%
Private infrastructure	0.24	0
Timberland	0.05	0
Private real estate debt	5.80	6
Private real estate equity	4.20	4
Public real estate equity	1.26	1
Commodities	0.33	0
Debt		
High-yield bonds	$1.85	2%
Bank loans	0.88	1
Emerging market bonds (sovereign, USD)	0.55	1
Emerging market bonds (sovereign, local foreign exchange)	1.48	1
Emerging market bonds (corporate, USD)	0.68	1
Insurance-linked securities	0.02	0
US bonds (investment grade)	15.34	15
Non-US bonds (developed)	22.65	22
Inflation-linked bonds	2.57	3
Money market/cash equivalents	4.49	4
Total global invested capital market	$101.10	100%

Note: Percentages do not add to 100% because of rounding.
Source: Hewitt EnnisKnupp, An Aon Company, "Global Invested Capital Market," Aon (June 2014): https://ctech.rproxy.hewitt.com/hig/filehandler.ashx?fileid=10355.

This industry guide will outline the organizational structure of the global asset management industry while providing perspective on some of the most important issues affecting asset managers (see **Figure 1**). Specifically, this guide will explore the following industry topics:

■ Portfolio management techniques

■ Major investor client segments and investment vehicles

■ Trends affecting the asset management industry

■ Key business metrics and financial statement considerations

Figure 1.   Asset Management Industry Structure

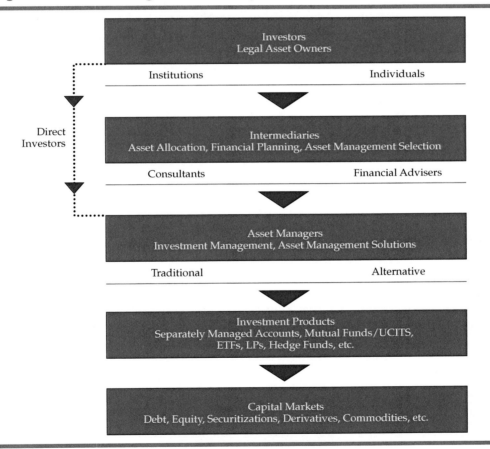

Note: UCITS are undertakings for the collective investment in transferable securities, ETFs are exchange-traded funds, and LPs are limited partners.

PORTFOLIO MANAGEMENT OVERVIEW

Professional investment portfolio management is the central service provided by asset managers. Asset managers typically act on behalf of investors, using investors' capital to implement investment strategies, and generally assume the role of a fiduciary—a guiding legal standard ensuring that asset managers act solely in the interests of investors and avoid conflicts of interest.

Although styles and techniques of portfolio management have continually shifted over time, in conjunction with capital market innovations and investor demand, investment strategies have generally been identified as either active or passive. Managers employing active techniques attempt to outperform (on an after-fee basis) predetermined performance benchmarks represented by relevant market indexes, such as the S&P 500 (large-capitalization US equities) or Barclays Global Aggregate Bond Index (global investment-grade fixed-rate debt). Active portfolio management represents the most prevalent form of portfolio management in the industry: In the United States, the world's largest asset management marketplace, approximately 73% of mutual fund assets were actively managed as of November 2013.[2]

Asset managers offering passive investment strategies attempt to replicate the returns of a market index largely by mirroring the index's holdings. Passive asset managers are measured by how closely they are able to track a market index—a process that is largely a function of index replication methodologies and asset management fees, which act as a permanent drag on returns for passive and active strategies alike.

ACTIVE PORTFOLIO MANAGEMENT

Asset managers employing active portfolio management techniques typically use a combination of *fundamental* and *quantitative* security selection methods to purchase a portfolio of securities that will, ideally, outperform a predetermined benchmark, often represented by a market index or absolute return goal (e.g., LIBOR plus 3%). Active portfolio management techniques encompass a broad range of methods used by research analysts and portfolio managers to ultimately form a view of a security's "intrinsic" value, as distinguished from the security's market value. Active

---

[2]Adam Zoll, "A Bull Market in Passive Investing," Morningstar (6 January 2014): http://ibd. morningstar.com/article/article.asp?id=624328&CN=brf295,http://ibd.morningstar.com/archive/archive.asp?inputs=days=14;frmtId=12,%20brf295.

managers believe capital markets offer opportunities to outperform market indexes and thus attempt to purchase securities or sectors perceived as "undervalued" in the market and, in some cases, short sell[3] securities deemed "overvalued." An active manager will vary weights on securities or sectors relative to their benchmark index weightings—overweighting undervalued securities and underweighting or negatively weighting (i.e., short selling) overvalued securities. In addition, managers often purchase securities not included in a benchmark index or focus their research efforts on less well-known companies—often unfollowed by sell-side research analysts—in an attempt to outperform a benchmark. Finally, managers of multi-asset and balanced strategies benchmarked to a static blend of equity and fixed-income indexes (e.g., 60% MSCI World Index, 40% Barclays Global Aggregate Bond Index) often vary exposures to asset classes (equities, bonds, currency) over either tactical (short-term) or strategic (long-term) time frames.

FUNDAMENTAL RESEARCH TECHNIQUES

Fundamental research requires both quantitative and analytical skills, as well as a dose of good judgment. Analysts and portfolio managers performing fundamental research typically collect financials and business metrics from required regulatory filings (e.g., in the United States, annual reports [10-Ks] and quarterly reports [10-Qs]), management presentations, sell-side investment research, data vendors, trade publications, and various other sources. With these research and financial inputs, the analyst or manager builds a security valuation model using a variety of discounting techniques based on projected earnings, dividends, and/or free cash flow. An analyst's valuation model is influenced by a qualitative view of a security's business and competitive prospects, which are often distilled from conversations with company management, vendors, customers, suppliers, and industry experts. Fundamental analysts and portfolio managers are often dedicated to research coverage of a single sector but may act as "generalists" covering multiple sectors. Given the growing importance to many companies of international revenues, more asset managers have begun to organize their sector research efforts on a global basis while deemphasizing the geographical domicile of the companies under their research coverage. For example, for Advanced Micro Devices, a semiconductor company based in Sunnyvale, California, generated international sales as a percentage of net revenue were 85% in 2013.[4]

---

[3]Short selling is the borrowing and subsequent selling of a security not owned by the seller that must later be returned, or "covered." The technique is used by investors aiming to profit from a security's price decline. Short-selling losses are theoretically unlimited but in practice are capped by margin maintenance rules imposed by brokerages.

[4]Advanced Micro Devices, "2013 Annual Report," AMD (March 2014): http://ir.amd.com/phoenix.zhtml?c= 74093&p=irol-reportsannual.

Global Industry Classification Standard

Established jointly by MSCI and Standard & Poor's, the Global Industry Classification Standard (GICS) is a widely used framework through which publicly traded companies are organized into comparable groups and subgroups. As of November 2014, the GICS structure consisted of 10 sectors, 24 industry groups, 67 industries, and 156 subindustries (see **Exhibit 1**).

Exhibit 1. Global Industry Classification Standard

Sector	Industry Group
Energy	■ Energy
Materials	■ Materials
Industrials	■ Capital goods
	■ Commercial and professional services
	■ Transportation
Consumer discretionary	■ Automobiles and components
	■ Consumer durables and apparel
	■ Hotels, restaurants, and leisure
	■ Media
	■ Retailing
Consumer staples	■ Food and staples retailing
	■ Food, beverage, and tobacco
	■ Household and personal products
Health care	■ Health care equipment and services
	■ Pharmaceuticals and biotechnology
Financials	■ Banks
	■ Diversified financials
	■ Insurance
	■ Real estate
Information technology	■ Software and services
	■ Technology hardware and equipment
	■ Semiconductors and semiconductor equipment
Telecommunication services	■ Telecommunication services
Utilities	■ Utilities

Source: MSCI, "GICS" (www.msci.com/products/indexes/sector/gics; retrieved 27 December 2014).

QUANTITATIVE TECHNIQUES

Quantitative portfolio management techniques are dispassionate and rely heavily on data, financial ratios, and statistical analysis to identify attractive securities. Analysts and portfolio managers—who often possess advanced quantitative and/or statistical training—seek to construct composites of "factors" ranging from financial data inputs to ratios (e.g., price/earnings, enterprise value/free cash flow, security price momentum), which are found to have historically significant relationships to security prices. Furthermore, factors incorporating fundamental-oriented judgments can be integrated into a quantitative process (e.g., sell-side analysts' earnings revisions and sell-side analyst performance ratings, such as those tracked by StarMine). Often, quantitative investment strategies rely on fundamental-based factors that possess a rational economic relationship to security prices and are designed to avoid spurious correlations.

In practice, most asset managers and portfolio management teams employ a combination of quantitative and fundamental analysis as a part of the investment process. However, from a business perspective, quantitative research methods are often considered more scalable and profitable than fundamental research methods because computing power is relatively inexpensive compared with the physical human capital required to expand fundamental security research coverage.

EQUITY PORTFOLIO MANAGEMENT

Equity investment strategies are managed in a variety of styles. Although some strategies focus on narrow niches of the equity universe, such as a specific sector (e.g., technology companies) or geographic exposure (e.g., emerging market equities), many are managed within specific guidelines defined by market capitalization and style (e.g., large-capitalization growth companies). "Unconstrained" equity strategies, which invest across a spectrum of global equities, have become increasingly common.

The global equity universe is valued at more than $62 trillion in market capitalization.[5] Within the equity universe, the United States represents the dominant exposure, as measured by the MSCI All Country World Index (ACWI), which covers 85% of the global investable equity universe, including 46 developed and emerging countries. **Table 2** and **Table 3** provide the country and sector weightings of the MSCI ACWI.[6]

---

[5]Weiyi Lim and Anna Kitanaka, "Global Stocks Erase 2014 Losses as $3 Trillion of Value Restored," *BloombergBusiness* (18 February 2014): www.bloomberg.com/news/2014-02-18/global-stocks-erase-2014-losses-as-3-trillion-of-value-restored.html.
[6]MSCI, "MSCI ACWI" (www.msci.com/resources/factsheets/index_fact_sheet/msci-acwi.pdf; retrieved 27 December 2014).

Table 2. MSCI ACWI: Country Weightings
(as of 30 June 2014)

Country	Weight
United States	48.9%
United Kingdom	7.8
Japan	7.4
Canada	3.9
France	3.7
Other	28.4

Table 3. MSCI ACWI: Sector Weightings
(as of 30 June 2014)

Sector	Weight
Financials	21.3%
Information technology	12.8
Consumer discretionary	11.6
Industrials	10.7
Health care	10.6
Energy	10.2
Consumer staples	9.6
Materials	6.1
Telecommunication services	3.9
Utilities	3.4

In the US mutual fund market alone, more than 7,500 distinct mutual funds are tracked by industry research and data supplier Morningstar.[7] To help simplify the many permutations of investment strategies that exist, many investors rely on a simple style box convention that arrays funds into a grid based on average market capitalization (large, mid, small) and investment style (value, core, growth). **Figure 2** illustrates the typical style box convention.

---

[7]Morningstar, "Morningstar Direct: Content and Data Quality" (http://corporate.morningstar.com/us/documents/MarketingFactSheets/ContentAndDataQualityFactsheet.pdf; retrieved 27 December 2014).

Figure 2. Equity Style Box Convention

		Investment Style		
		Value ■ Low P/E ■ High Dividend Yield	Core ■ Mid P/E ■ Mid Dividend Yield	Growth ■ High P/E ■ Low Dividend Yield
Market Capitalization	*Large* > $10 billion			
	Mid $2 billion–$10 billion			
	Small $250 million– $2 billion			

Equities are generally categorized along a continuum ranging from value to growth. Value companies tend to exhibit certain common characteristics: low price-to-earnings, price-to-book, and enterprise-value-to-EBITDA ratios and high dividend yields. Growth companies tend to exhibit opposite metrics relative to their value counterparts and generally avoid dividends because retained earnings are reinvested in capital or research and development projects. Core, or blend, equities share characteristics of both value and growth groups. In practice, significant qualitative judgment is applied to each of these categorizations and different portfolio managers can form very divergent views as to the same security.

Equity categories are not exclusively limited to delineations along market capitalization and style lines. Industry data providers have formed dozens of investment categories that span regions, asset classes, sectors, and investment strategy styles.

The use of investment categories allows investors to create appropriate peer groups to evaluate the relative performance and product characteristics (e.g., fees, investment guidelines) of similar investment strategies offered by different asset managers. In addition, investors benefit from being able to construct diversified portfolios that avoid potentially duplicative allocations to similar securities.

Exhibit 2 outlines a version of the investment guidelines a typical institutional investor would require of an asset manager managing a US large-capitalization blend strategy benchmarked to the S&P 500.

Exhibit 2. Domestic US Large-Cap Equity Portfolio: Sample Investment Guidelines

Investment objective

- Outperform the S&P 500 after fees by 100 bps over a market cycle
- Generate excess returns with an information ratio of at least 0.25

Risk management (maximum limitations)

- 125% of sector's index weighting
- 35% in any one sector
- 7% in any one holding or 1.5× security's index weighting
- 7% cash position
- 2% ownership of any one corporation's common shares
- 10% preferred securities

Sovereign risk

- 20% non-US securities (American Depositary Receipts and US-listed securities only)
- 7% in any other country

Liquidity risk

- 80% of portfolio must be in securities traded on a major exchange
- Private placements, physical real estate, and commodities prohibited

Source: Public School Employees' Retirement System, "Pennsylvania Public School Employees' Retirement System Investment Objectives and Guidelines: U.S. Style-Oriented Large Cap Equities, Addendum A" (9 December 2011): www.psers.state.pa.us/content/investments/guidelines/A%20(approved%202011-12-09).pdf.

FIXED-INCOME PORTFOLIO MANAGEMENT

Fixed-income portfolio management requires many of the same fundamental analytical skills used in equity portfolio management; however, a distinct analytical skill set and viewpoint are also required. Fixed-income securities typically feature an asymmetric risk profile because an investor's upside return potential is generally limited to predefined coupons and the return of principal, whereas downside potential may extend to a default scenario in which only a fraction of principal is recovered.

Fixed-income portfolios typically include diverse exposures to either taxable or tax-exempt fixed-income securities categorized in five broad classifications: government-issued securities, inflation-indexed securities, corporate securities, mortgage-backed securities, and asset-backed securities (e.g., credit cards, auto loans, licensing fees). The Barclays Global Aggregate Index provides a view of the global investment-grade fixed-income universe of 24 countries. **Figure 3** and **Figure 4** provide a historical view of the Barclays Global Aggregate Index's sector and quality composition.

Actively managed bond strategies employ a number of techniques to add value relative to an index. The most common techniques that fixed-income portfolio managers employ include duration management, maturity structure management, sector management, credit and risk spread management, and yield curve positioning.

Figure 3. Barclays Global Aggregate Index: Sector Composition (as of March 2014)

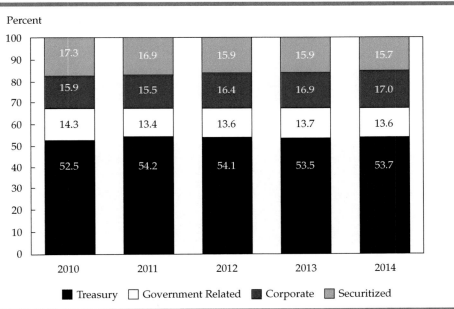

Source: Barclays, "Global Aggregate Index" (https://index.barcap.com/Home/Guides_and_Factsheets; retrieved 27 December 2014).

Figure 4. Barclays Global Aggregate Index: Quality Composition (as of March 2014)

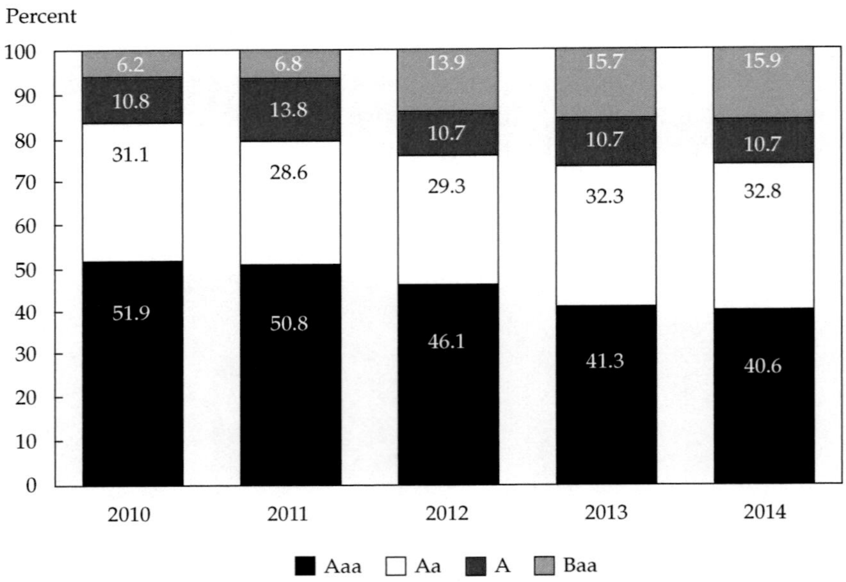

Percent

Year	Aaa	Aa	A	Baa
2010	51.9	31.1	10.8	6.2
2011	50.8	28.6	13.8	6.8
2012	46.1	29.3	10.7	13.9
2013	41.3	32.3	10.7	15.7
2014	40.6	32.8	10.7	15.9

■ Aaa □ Aa ■ A ▨ Baa

Source: Barclays, "Global Aggregate Index" (https://index.barcap.com/Home/Guides_and_Factsheets; retrieved 27 December 2014).

DURATION MANAGEMENT

Increasing or decreasing a bond portfolio's duration is a key lever for portfolio managers seeking to act on the projected path of interest rates.[8] In anticipation of increasing interest rates, managers will shorten duration to limit price declines; conversely, managers will lengthen duration when rates are anticipated to decline. The strong influence of central banks on the path of interest rates during and following the 2008 financial crisis highlighted the importance of understanding the investment implications of central bank policy.

---

[8]In its simplest form, duration is an approximate measure—expressed in years—of a bond's price sensitivity to a change in interest rates. Duration measures the approximate percentage change in a bond's price resulting from a 1% change in its yield. An inverse relationship exists between bond prices and interest rates.

YIELD CURVE STRUCTURE MANAGEMENT

Managers anticipating future shifts in the shape of the yield curve can alter a portfolio's maturity structure to take advantage of such shifts. In the case of a flattening of the yield curve—when interest rates rise at the short end while falling on the long end—a manager would benefit from a "barbell" approach that weights a portfolio's assets both toward the short end of the curve to benefit from higher reinvestment rates and toward the long end of the curve to capture bond price appreciation driven by lower rates.

SECTOR EXPOSURE

Portfolio managers often shift sector weightings relative to a benchmark index based on their expectations regarding relative sector performance. For example, a portfolio manager anticipating deteriorating credit fundamentals among financial services companies will underweight the portfolio's exposure to financials relative to the benchmark index to achieve excess relative returns. A manager expecting a general recession will increase allocations to "risk-free" Treasuries.

CREDIT SPREAD AND RISK MANAGEMENT

Assessing credit risk (i.e., the probability of a company being able to meet its contractually obligated interest and principal payments) is the primary objective of credit analysis (see **Exhibit 3**). Managers can add value by investing in undervalued credits and avoiding the debt securities of companies expected to face significant business or default risk. Managers also attempt to anticipate the tightening and expansion of credit spreads between Treasuries and non-Treasuries by shifting exposures between investment and high-yield credits.

Trading liquidity in the bond market is a critical factor to consider. Unlike most equity securities, which trade on organized exchanges (both physical and electronic), bonds trade "over the counter" via dispersed dealer networks. Without a centralized quotation system, bond pricing tends to be inconsistent and bonds are often priced differently by different agencies. Liquidity considerations are especially salient in the municipal bond market, where in 2011, for example, approximately 99% of outstanding municipal securities did not trade on any given day.[9]

Many investors use a simple style box convention that arrays bond funds in a grid based on average maturity (short, intermediate, long) and credit quality (investment grade, high yield). **Figure 5** summarizes the typical fixed-income style box convention.

---

[9]SEC, "Report on the Municipal Securities Market," US Securities and Exchange Commission (31 July 2012): www.sec.gov/news/studies/2012/munireport073112.pdf.

Exhibit 3. Credit Ratings Summary by Rating Agency

Moody's Investors Service	S&P	Fitch Ratings	Description
Investment grade			
Aaa	AAA	AAA	Prime
Aa	AA	AA	High grade
A	A	A	Upper medium grade
Baa	BBB	BBB	Lower medium grade/crossover
Below investment grade			
Ba	BB	BB	Speculative
B	B	B	Highly speculative
Caa	CCC	CCC	Extremely speculative
Ca	CC	CCC	Default imminent
C	D	D	In default

Figure 5. Fixed-Income Style Box Convention

		Average Credit Quality	
		Investment-Grade S&P Ratings AAA–BBB	High-Yield S&P Ratings BB–D
Duration	*Short* 1–3 years		
	Intermediate 5–7 years		
	Long +10 years		

The portfolio guideline structure for a domestic investment-grade core fixed-income investment strategy for a typical institutional investor (based in the United States) is detailed in **Exhibit 4**.

Exhibit 4. Core Fixed-Income Portfolio: Sample

Investment objective

- Outperform the Barclays Capital US Aggregate Bond Index (BC Aggregate) over a complete market cycle (three to five years)
- Maintain +/– two-year duration versus the BC Aggregate

Risk management

- Portfolio average credit rating of at least A; lowest rating for an individual security BBB– (S&P)
- Minimum of 25 issuers, 10% max weight in a single issuer
- 10% max cash allocation
- No leverage
- No short selling

Sovereign risk

- 10% in non-dollar-denominated bonds
- 15% in US-dollar-denominated issues from foreign governments and corporations

MULTI-ASSET PORTFOLIOS

Managing portfolios across equities and fixed-income securities in a single investment strategy is commonplace with many investment managers. Multi-asset strategies come in many types, ranging from simple balanced strategies that maintain a fixed allocation to equities and bonds (e.g., a 60% equity, 40% fixed-income strategy with quarterly rebalancing) to global asset allocation strategies that rely heavily on macro-level forecasts to allocate assets across geographies and asset classes, including equities, fixed income, and "real assets," such as commodities and real estate.

One of the fastest-growing segments of the "multi-asset" space is target-date mutual funds, which represent diversified portfolio investment solutions designed for retirement investors. Typically, these funds gradually shift asset allocation exposures over time from an equity-centric asset allocation at the outset of an investor's time horizon to a more conservative, fixed-income posture to coincide with an investor's expected retirement date. The turnkey nature of these funds has caused them to be widely adopted in the employer-sponsored defined contribution (DC) marketplace in the United States (see the Industry Trends section) and other jurisdictions as well.

MONEY MARKET FUNDS

First introduced in the 1970s, money market mutual funds are a mainstay investment for US individuals and institutions: They held more than $2.6 trillion in assets under management (AUM), representing 17% of US mutual fund assets, as of year-end 2013. Money market mutual funds are a key investment offering for many asset managers, and though uninsured in the United States, they often represent a substitute for several retail bank offerings (e.g., savings accounts). Most money market funds are designed to maintain a $1/share net asset value (NAV) by investing in high-quality, short-term debt securities, including US Treasuries, agencies, certificates of deposits, commercial paper, and repos (repurchase agreements).[10] In order to report a stable $1/share NAV, asset managers in the United States must comply with Rule 2a-7, an SEC regulation that imposes a number of portfolio limitations on money market funds, including the following:

- Securities must have maturities of less than 397 days.

- Average portfolio maturity must be less than 60 days.

- At least 10% of a portfolio must be invested in cash or convertible into cash within a day; 30% must be similarly liquid within a week.

- Securities must have short-term ratings within the two highest tiers from nationally recognized statistical rating organizations.

During the 2008 financial crisis, money market funds took center stage as the $68 billion Reserve Primary Fund became the second money market fund in the industry to "break the buck" after suffering $785 million in losses on Lehman Brothers debt. The loss caused the fund's NAV to dip to $0.97 per share and prompted a wave of investor redemptions as fear of future losses mounted. Ultimately, the Federal Reserve helped to assuage investor fears by establishing a $600 billion liquidity backstop called the "Money Market Investor Funding Facility."[11] The Fed introduced its liquidity facility—which ultimately was never tapped—after asset managers had already put up more than $10 billion to support redemptions.[12]

---

[10]The SEC permits only money market funds subject to Rule 2a-7 to use amortized cost accounting for reporting the NAV, which affords these funds the ability to offer and redeem shares at $1/share. The SEC also requires money market funds to maintain a "shadow" NAV, which is based on market values. Money market funds that fall in value by more than one-half cent per share are said to have "broken the buck" and begin to report NAVs based on market value.

[11]Board of Governors of the Federal Reserve System, "Money Market Investor Funding Facility (MMIFF)," Federal Reserve (www.federalreserve.gov/newsevents/reform_mmiff.htm).

[12]Eric Dash, "Rethinking Money Market Funds," *New York Times* (11 July 2008).

The Reserve Primary Fund experience helped spawn new rules in the United States, adopted in 2010, which tightened the liquidity and holdings requirements of money market funds. On 23 July 2014, the SEC introduced additional regulation pertaining to money market funds. The new rules require institutional prime money market funds—those generally used by corporations—to float NAVs rather than maintain stable $1/share NAVs. In addition, if certain asset threshold tests are met, the SEC will grant mutual fund boards broader power to impose gates or redemption fees (up to 2%) on money market redemptions. Money market funds used by retail investors will continue to maintain a stable $1/share NAV.

INDEX PORTFOLIO MANAGEMENT

Index providers, such as Russell, Barclays, Standard & Poor's, and MSCI, calculate and maintain thousands of benchmark indexes that track asset classes across the capital spectrum. An index can be created for virtually any market, provided the underlying securities included in the index possess adequate liquidity and quoted prices. Index managers typically employ full replication or sampling methods to replicate the performance of benchmark indexes.

FULL REPLICATION

The most straightforward index replication strategy exactly matches an index's constituents. For example, the manager of the XYZ S&P 500 Index Fund will own all 500 stocks listed in the S&P 500 Index. This technique is common for indexes tracking large, liquid segments of the market, such as large-cap stocks.

SAMPLING

Sampling, or optimization, techniques attempt to replicate the performance of an index without using the full complement of securities contained in the index. Through the use of statistical modeling, a manager attempts to replicate the performance of an index by approximating its risk factors, such as sector allocations, portfolio duration, and maturity profile. Asset managers typically use sampling techniques when replicating bond indexes, given the large number of securities and liquidity constraints associated with most fixed-income indexes. The Barclays US Aggregate Index includes more than 8,000 securities; however, the iShares Core US Aggregate Bond ETF (exchange-traded fund) uses 2,795 holdings to replicate the performance of the Barclays index.[13]

---

[13]BlackRock, "iShares Core U.S. Aggregate Bond ETF" (www.ishares.com/us/literature/fact-sheet/agg-ishares-core-u-s-aggregate-bond-etf-fund-fact-sheet-en-us.pdf; retrieved 29 December 2014).

Index strategies are intended to replicate the underlying returns of a market benchmark. Theoretically, an index strategy that perfectly tracks its benchmark will underperform by an amount equal to the total expenses associated with managing the strategy, including management, operational, and trading fees. Asset managers offering the lowest-cost index strategies have attracted significant investor interest.

The results of index-tracking strategies are typically measured in terms of tracking error. Tracking error represents the volatility of the difference between a manager's returns and the returns of the benchmark. The smaller the tracking error value, the more closely a manager is replicating the benchmark. Many large index asset managers operate securities lending programs whereby managers lend index securities to other investors (typically short sellers) in return for a fee. The revenue earned from this activity, if implemented successfully, is typically shared with investors and helps to offset operating expenses and reduce tracking error.

INDEX WEIGHTING METHODOLOGIES

Most of the investing world's widely followed equity and fixed-income market indexes are market-capitalization weighted, including the S&P 500 and the Barclays US Aggregate Bond Index. A market-cap-weighted index simply weights each component security in proportion to its capitalization in the general market. Therefore, the largest component securities by market capitalization form the largest components of the index, and thus, the index reflects the "market." The performance of individual securities and sectors can have a material impact on the performance of an index. A recent market example demonstrates this point: At the height of the US technology boom during the 1990s, the technology sector had a weighting in the S&P 500/ BARRA Growth Index of more than 50%, compared with its historical average of less than 20% (see **Figure 6**).

Asset managers have recently begun to address the perceived weaknesses of market-cap-weighted indexes by introducing products that rely on alternative weighting schemes (e.g., index weightings determined by a combination of "attractive" fundamental characteristics, dividend yield, etc.) and/or inclusion rules. The asset managers marketing these alternatively weighted indexes often describe them as "smart beta" or "enhanced beta" strategies.

Figure 6. S&P 500/BARRA Growth Index

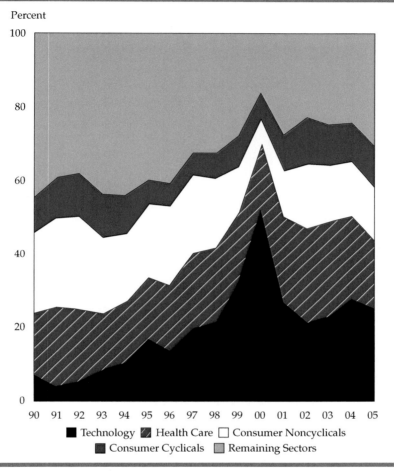

Source: William Hester, "Large Value Index Bets Big on Economic Growth and Financials," Hussman Funds (July 2005): www.hussmanfunds.com/rsi/lgvaluebets.htm.

TRADITIONAL VS. ALTERNATIVE ASSET MANAGERS

Asset managers are typically categorized as either "traditional" or "alternative." Traditional managers derive the majority of their revenues from asset-based fees and generally focus their efforts on long-only equity, fixed-income, and multi-asset investment strategies. Alternative asset managers—including hedge fund, private equity (PE), and venture capital managers—rely heavily on management and performance fees (or "carried interest") to generate revenue. Although PE and venture capital firms typically pursue private market transactions, hedge funds typically trade in mainstream and more exotic corners of the public markets and often employ derivatives and short-selling techniques. Many alternative managers also use financial leverage (e.g., bank borrowing) to enhance the returns of investment strategies.

Increasingly, the line between "alternative" and "traditional" managers is blurring as traditional managers seek to deliver higher-margin alternative products to retail segments of the market (see the Franklin Templeton Investments case study later). Concurrently, alternative managers seeking to reduce the revenue volatility associated with performance fees and carried interest (performance fees are inherently less predictable than recurring management fee revenue) are increasingly offering retail versions of their alternative strategies (featuring less leverage, no performance fees, and more liquid holdings), in addition to offering long-only investment strategies that generate more stable asset-based fees. The Blackstone Group, the world's largest PE manager, recently launched a multistrategy mutual fund (ticker symbol BXMMX) for retail investors via Fidelity Investments' distribution network. In addition, Blackstone partnered with State Street Global Advisors to manage an ETF focused on non-investment-grade senior bank loans (ticker symbol SRLN).

HEDGE FUNDS

The hedge fund is a mid-20th-century US financial invention, and today's hedge funds represent one of the most important segments of the asset management industry; having eclipsed their 2007 peak, assets stood at $2.2 trillion as of 31 March 2014. Hedge funds generally play a supporting role in an investor's asset allocation as a portfolio diversifier, alongside core allocations to long-only equity and fixed-income strategies. Hedge funds represent a broad set of investment styles and strategies but generally share a few distinguishing characteristics:

- *Short selling.* Profiting from a decline in a security's price is a hallmark of most hedge fund strategies. Portfolio managers can implement short sales to profit from price declines of individual securities, sectors, and/or broad market indexes. Shorts are implemented directly or synthetically through the use of derivatives, such as options, futures, and credit default swaps.

- *Absolute return seeking.* Although traditional long-only investment strategies aim to provide investment returns relative to a benchmark—seeking to outperform a benchmark index in positive return environments and lose less than the benchmark in negative market environments—the goal of absolute return investing is to pursue positive returns in all market environments over a market cycle.

- *Leverage.* A number of hedge fund styles call for the use of financial leverage (bank borrowing) or implicit leverage (through the use of derivatives, such as options, swaps, and futures) to magnify the impact of relatively small profit-making opportunities. The use of leverage and the amount of leverage employed are highly dependent on the investment strategy being implemented (see **Table 4**).

- *Low correlation.* Many investors look to hedge funds to provide a form of portfolio ballast in volatile market environments because hedge funds have historically exhibited low return correlations with traditional asset classes (see **Table 5**).

- *Fee structures.* Hedge funds typically charge two layers of fees: a traditional asset-based management fee—calculated as a percentage of AUM—and a performance fee, which allocates a percentage of the fund's realized capital gains to the asset manager.[14] Hedge funds have traditionally charged management fees of 2% and performance fees of up to 20%, although managers have witnessed downward pressure on those fees because of growing investor resistance.

---

[14]Performance fees are often subject to high-water mark provisions, which preclude a manager from earning a performance fee unless the value of a fund at the end of a predefined measurement period is higher than the value of the fund at the beginning of the measurement period. The unpredictability of future performance leads to uncertainty in performance fee revenue, which is regarded as less reliable than revenue derived from management fees.

Table 4. Leverage by Hedge Fund Strategy

Strategy	Leverage Guidelines	
	Typical	Max
Convertible arbitrage	4×	6×
Distressed debt	1	1.5
Event-driven equity and merger arbitrage	1.3	2
Fixed-income arbitrage	8	15
Global macro	5	10
Long–short equity, fundamental	1.3	2
Long–short equity, quantitative	2.5	5
Multistrategy	3.5	6

Source: Frank Barbarino, "Leverage, Hedge Funds and Risk," NEPC (Summer 2009): www.nepc.com/writable/research_articles/file/09_07_nepc_leverage_hf_and_risk.pdf.

Table 5. Hedge Fund Strategy Correlations with Equities and Bonds

Jan. 1990 to Jan. 2014	Developed Market Equities	Developed Government Bonds	Event-Driven Index	Equity Hedge Index	Equity Market Neutral Index	Quantitative Directional	Macro Index	Relative Value Index
Developed market equities	1.00							
Developed government bonds	−0.01	1.00						
Event-driven index	0.61	−0.09	1.00					
Equity hedge index	0.63	−0.05	0.84	1.00				
Equity market neutral index	0.16	0.04	0.42	0.51	1.00			
Quantitative directional	0.71	−0.02	0.82	0.89	0.34	1.00		
Macro index	0.34	0.35	0.51	0.55	0.34	0.55	1.00	
Relative value index	0.41	−0.05	0.77	0.68	0.41	0.57	0.34	1.00

Source: Adam J. Eisenberg and David Doberman, "Alternative Trading Strategies: Opportunities in Long/Short Equity," Barclays (25 March 2014): https://wealth.barclays.com/en_gb/home/research/research-centre/compass/compass-mar-214/opportunities-in-long-short-equity.html.

Hedge fund investment strategies are diverse and can range from highly specific niche strategies (e.g., long–short financial services) to global multistrategy approaches that employ multiple techniques across global capital markets. **Exhibit 5** provides an overview of several major categories of hedge fund investment strategies.

Hedge fund industry AUM have grown steadily as the use of hedge funds has expanded among institutional investors. **Table 6** lists the 10 largest hedge fund managers.

Exhibit 5. Overview of Major Hedge Fund Strategies

Strategy	Description
Global macro	Focuses on implementing macroeconomic bets on such factors as interest rates, currencies, and relative country/market performance. Managers often employ derivatives to quickly enter and exit positions (both long and short).
Equity long–short	Profits from long (undervalued) and short (overvalued) positions in equities. Net market exposure can be adjusted based on overall market direction or prevalence of attractive long–short candidates, or exposure can be kept beta neutral to isolate stock-specific risk. Some managers hedge beta risk purely by shorting market indexes rather than individual companies.
Distressed	Involves the purchase of securities (debt, equity, convertibles, etc.) of companies in or approaching bankruptcy. Returns tend to be uncorrelated with market conditions because the returns are based on events specific to the distressed company—negotiations among creditors, divestiture proceedings, etc. Managers often commit significant legal resources when analyzing investment opportunities.
Event driven	A broad set of strategies designed to profit from corporate events, including mergers and acquisitions, bankruptcies, and spinoffs. Merger arbitrage trades attempt to profit from spreads between takeover offers and the market price of a target's securities. In the context of a cash-financed merger, a portfolio manager will acquire shares of the target company, which often trade below the offer price, in return for assuming the risk that a deal will not reach completion. Leverage is often employed to magnify merger arbitrage returns.
Managed futures	Relies primarily on the use of futures contracts to take long and short positions across a multitude of commodity, interest rate, and other financial futures markets. Many managed futures strategies rely on quantitative management techniques designed to identify short-term price and momentum trends in futures contracts across markets.
Multistrategy	A single fund or fund-of-funds strategy designed to combine multiple hedge fund investment strategies in a single fund. Often, multiple specialist asset managers are engaged to individually manage each substrategy within a fund-of-funds strategy. Fund-of-funds managers charge an overlay fee (often a 1% management fee plus 10% of profits) in addition to the expenses charged by the underlying hedge fund managers.

Table 6. Largest Hedge Fund Managers
(as of 31 March 2014, $ billions)

Manager	AUM
Bridgewater Associates	$87.1
J.P. Morgan Asset Management	59.0
Brevan Howard	40.0
Och-Ziff Capital Management	36.1
BlueCrest Capital Management	32.6
BlackRock	31.3
AQR Capital Management	29.9
Lone Pine Capital	29.0
Man Group	28.3
Viking Global Investors	27.1

Source: Sital S. Patel, "Bridgewater, J.P. Morgan Top List of 100 Largest Hedge Funds," MarketWatch (12 May 2014): http://blogs.marketwatch.com/thetell/2014/05/12/bridgewater-j-p-morgan-top-list-of-100-largest-hedge-funds.

PRIVATE EQUITY AND VENTURE CAPITAL

As of June 2013, the PE industry's AUM topped $3.5 trillion, inclusive of uncalled capital commitments and unrealized value of portfolio assets.[15] Private equity and venture capital managers (general partners, or GPs) generally operate in a similar manner, raising investor capital (capital commitments) from investors (limited partners, or LPs) to buy, optimize, and ultimately sell portfolio companies to generate profits. Although LPs commit the majority of a fund's capital, GPs also commit approximately 1%–5% of the fund's capital to help align their interests with those of the LP investors. Most PE funds have a defined lifespan of approximately 7–10 years (usually subject to contractual extensions) and spend the first few years acquiring 10 or more attractive target companies, applying many of the same fundamental research techniques described previously. Unlike most traditional asset managers trading in public securities, PE and venture firms often take a hands-on approach to their portfolio companies through a combination of financial engineering (e.g., realizing expense synergies, changes to the capital stack), the installation of their own executives and board members, and significant contributions to the development of a target firm's business strategy. The final stage, often referred to as the "harvesting"

---

[15]Preqin, "2014 Preqin Global Private Equity Report, Sample Pages" (www.preqin.com/docs/samples/The_2014_Preqin_Global_Private_Equity_Report_Sample_Pages.pdf; retrieved 27 December 2014).

or "exit" phase, occurs when a fund begins to profitably divest its portfolio companies through an IPO, a private sale to a competitor ("strategic buyer"), or a sale to another PE firm. **Figure 7** illustrates the typical return pattern for PE.

PE firms generate revenue through several means:

■ *Management fees*: AUM-based fees (1%–2%) calculated on committed capital that sometimes step down several years into the investment period of a fund or are calculated based on net invested capital.

■ *Transaction and monitoring fees*: Fees paid by portfolio companies to the GP for various corporate and structuring services. Typically, a percentage of this fee revenue reverts back to the LPs in the form of management fee offsets.

■ *Investment income*: Gains generated on capital contributed to the fund by the GP.

■ *Carried interest*: Represents the GP's share of gains (typically 20%) on sales of portfolio companies. The distribution of proceeds from portfolio company sales is subject to specific "distribution waterfall" terms. In a European-style waterfall, GPs collect fees only after LPs receive distributions equal to their committed capital plus a preferred or hurdle return (typically about 5%–8%). A GP "catch-up" may exist in some instances in which the GP is allocated 100% of the distributions until it has received 20% of the distributions in

Figure 7. Private Equity: J Curve Return Pattern

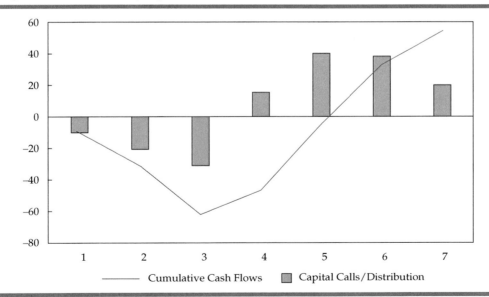

excess of return of capital. After clearing the preferred return to LPs and the GP catch-up, all remaining distributions follow the normal 80/20 split carried interest allocation. It is important to note that if a fund's performance turns negative, "clawback" terms—contractual provisions that define the terms under which carried interest is refunded to LPs—can become relevant to certain distribution waterfall structures in which carried interest is calculated on a deal-by-deal basis.

Institutional investors have long been attracted to the returns generated by private strategies relative to the public markets. Consider, for example, the largest PE managers (see **Table 7**). Over the last 20 years, PE funds have outperformed the S&P 500 by more than 400 bps on an annualized, net-of-fees basis (see **Table 8**). That said, the dispersion of returns between top-quartile and bottom-quartile performing managers has historically been quite high, implying that proper manager selection is a critical consideration for PE investors. In addition, gaining access to top-performing managers and achieving desired commitment sizes have become increasingly difficult for institutional investors.

Table 7. Largest PE Managers, Five-Year Fundraising Totals
(as of March 2014, $ billions)

Manager	AUM
The Carlyle Group	$30.7
Kohlberg Kravis Roberts	27.2
The Blackstone Group	24.6
Apollo Global Management	22.3
TPG	18.8
CVC Capital Partners	16.6
General Atlantic	16.6
Ares Management	14.1
Clayton Dubilier & Rice	13.5
Advent International	13.2

Source: "The Ten Biggest Private Equity Firms in the World," GrowthBusiness (2 May 2014): www.growthbusiness.co.uk/news-and-market-deals/business-news/2462432/the-ten-biggest-private-equity-firms-in-the-world.thtml.

Table 8. US Private Equity and Venture Capital Index Returns
(as of Q1 2014)

Index	1-Year	3-Year	5-Year	10-Year	15-Year	20-Year	25-Year
Cambridge Associates US Private Equity	19.1%	14.2%	17.4%	14%	12%	13.7%	13.7%
Cambridge Associates US Venture Capital	30.5	15.3	14.1	10	18.7	31.7	21.1
Dow Jones Industrial Average	15.7	13	19.9	7.5	6	10.3	10.9
NASDAQ Composite	28.5	14.7	22.4	7.7	3.6	9	9.8
Russell 2000	24.9	13.2	24.3	8.5	8.9	9.5	9.9
S&P 500	21.9	14.7	21.2	7.4	4.5	9.5	10

Source: Cambridge Associates, "U.S. Private Equity Index and Selected Benchmark Statistics" (31 March 2014): http://40926u2govf9kuqen1ndit018su.wpengine.netdna-cdn.com/wp-content/uploads/2014/07/Public-USPE-Benchmark-2014-Q1.pdf.

**Alternative Asset Manager Profile:
Kohlberg Kravis Roberts & Co.**

OVERVIEW

Founded in 1976 by Henry Kravis and George Roberts, Kohlberg Kravis Roberts & Co. (KKR) is one of the oldest and most recognized alternative investment firms operating in the United States. Throughout the firm's history, its PE business has completed more than 230 PE investments, many via leveraged buyouts, with a total transaction value of more than $485 billion. The firm is widely known for completing one of the largest leverage buyouts in history with its purchase of RJR Nabisco in 1988. KKR became a public company and listed on the NYSE on 15 July 2010.

BUSINESS SEGMENTS

KKR operates three main business lines: Private Markets, Public Markets, and Capital Markets.

Private Markets. PE represents KKR's primary business line with more than $62 billion in AUM as of 31 March 2014. Also as of that date, KKR held 93 portfolio companies across 16 industries. Collectively, these portfolio companies generate more than $200 billion in annual revenue and employ more than 940,000 people (see, for example, Table 1).

KKR's historical PE business has generated substantial profits for its limited partners. The firm has collectively posted a 26% gross internal rate of return on its funds, outperforming the S&P 500 by more than 700 bps.

Public Markets. KKR's Public Markets business manages more than $42 billion in assets via credit and hedge funds. Through its registered investment adviser affiliates, the firm manages a variety of traditional debt strategies focused on high-yield bonds and leveraged loans. In addition, KKR manages a number of alternative credit strategies, including mezzanine financing, long–short credit, distressed credit, and direct lending to middle-market companies seeking financing.

Capital Markets. Via affiliated broker/dealers, KKR's Capital Markets division provides a variety of capital market and traditional investment banking services to both its portfolio and third-party companies. Services include equity and debt arranging and underwriting and IPOs/follow-ons. The firm's principal activities involve using the firm's own balance sheet to make investments in its funds and to co-invest in certain portfolio companies. KKR uses its investments as seed capital and to increase its participation in funds, aligning its interests with those of limited partners.

Sources: KKR, "Annual Report" (2013): http://ir.kkr.com/kkr_ir/kkr_annuals.cfm; KKR, "Investor Presentation" (November 2014): http://ir.kkr.com/kkr_ir/kkr_events.cfm.

REAL ESTATE AND INFRASTRUCTURE

REAL ESTATE

Private real estate debt and equity assets are considered the most ubiquitous alternative assets, accounting for approximately half of global alternative assets (see Table 1). Direct and indirect investments in such assets as land, single-family housing, multifamily housing, and urban office properties have long been a mainstay for investors. Real estate assets have generally featured low correlations with equities and fixed income and are considered long-term assets that yield relatively stable cash flows, often positively correlated with inflation. **Table 9** lists the 10 largest real estate managers.

Table 9. **Largest Real Estate Managers**
(as of year-end 2012, $ billions)

Manager	AUM
Brookfield Asset Management	$115.4
CBRE Global Investors	90.7
The Blackstone Group	88.6
UBS Global Asset Management	64.7
AXA Real Estate	59.6
J.P. Morgan Asset Management	55.9
TIAA-CREF Asset Management	55.2
Prudential Real Estate Investors	52.2
Invesco Real Estate	50.6
Deutsche Asset & Wealth Management	48.7

Source: Property Funds Research and Institutional Real Estate, "Global Investment Managers 2013," Institutional Real Estate (2013): www.irei.com/userfiles/cms/investmentManagerReport/1/2013pfr-ireireportus.pdf.

INFRASTRUCTURE

Investing in infrastructure-related assets (e.g., bridges, tunnels, power generation, and waste management facilities) continues to grow among institutional investors seeking to secure relatively reliable long-term yields with a degree of inflation protection. As the gap between required infrastructure spending and public funding continues to widen, opportunities have expanded for private investment to provide financing.

MAJOR ASSET MANAGEMENT CLIENT SEGMENTS

Asset managers serve two broad client segments: retail investors and institutional investors. The segmentation of these channels is the result of the varying distribution, product, and client-servicing needs. Asset managers targeting retail investors typically package investment strategies through highly regulated collective investment vehicles (CIVs), legally referred to as "investment companies"[16] in the United States, and possess a large distribution staff geared toward either "wholesaling" products through financial advisers or reaching investors directly. Institutionally focused managers often market directly to large institutional clients or to investment consultants, and they typically package their investment strategies in less regulated and more customizable product structures, including separately managed accounts and limited partnerships. Many institutionally focused asset managers that do not possess a retail distribution presence opt to pursue the retail channel through subadvisory relationships. Through a subadvisory relationship, a retail-focused asset manager essentially subcontracts the investment management responsibilities of a collective investment vehicle—typically a mutual fund or undertakings for the collective investment in transferable securities (UCITS)—to a third-party institutional asset manager while retaining distribution and marketing responsibility for the fund. The relationship allows a retail asset manager to offer its clients access to an institutionally focused asset manager while providing an expanded distribution and revenue opportunity for the institutional manager.

---

[16]The SEC defines an investment company as "a company (corporation, business trust, partnership, or limited liability company) that issues securities and is primarily engaged in the business of investing in securities" (Investment Company Act of 1940). US federal securities law recognizes three types of investment companies: mutual funds, closed-end funds, and unit investment trusts.

RETAIL INVESTORS

UNITED STATES

Asset managers participating in the retail channel typically sell funds directly to investors on a wholesale basis—through financial advisers acting on an investor's behalf and through defined contribution (DC) plans—for example, 401(k)s. Asset managers targeting financial advisers, or "intermediaries," face a diverse community encompassing more than 300,000 advisers in the United States.[17] The major US distribution channels within the intermediary space include national full-service broker/dealers, often referred to as "wire houses" (e.g., Morgan Stanley Wealth Management, Bank of America Merrill Lynch, UBS, and Wells Fargo); regional broker/dealers with a concentrated geographical presence (e.g., RBC Wealth Management, Janney Montgomery Scott); independent broker/dealers with a national presence whose advisers are generally independent contractors rather than employees (e.g., LPL Financial, Ameriprise, Raymond James); and insurance-affiliated broker/dealers (e.g., MetLife, AIG Advisor Group).

Registered investment advisers (RIAs) represent a distinct retail distribution channel. RIAs are regulated by the SEC or relevant state(s) (rather than the Financial Industry Regulatory Authority, which regulates most broker/dealers), and they charge clients asset-based fees for "advice" rather than commissions. RIAs have a legal fiduciary obligation to their clients, requiring that they always act in the best interests of their clients, whereas most other advisers are held to the less rigorous standard of "suitability." Many RIAs clear and custody their assets through national clearing firms, such as Charles Schwab, National Financial Services (owned by Fidelity), and Pershing.

Many asset managers access self-directed investors by establishing distribution agreements with major online brokerage firms, such as Fidelity, Charles Schwab, TD Ameritrade, Vanguard, and E*TRADE.

Table 10 provides an overview of the US retail investment market by distribution channel, showing projected growth over the next five years.

---

[17]Andrew Osterland, "Advisors Slow to Train Successors," CNBC (1 May 2014): www.cnbc.com/id/101621040#.

Table 10. US Retail Distribution Channels

Distribution Channel	Approximate Share of Mutual Fund AUM	Forecasted 5-Year Compound Annual Growth Rate (CAGR)
National wire houses	21%	4.8%
Independent advisers	10	5.9
RIAs	13	10.4
Regional broker/dealers	9	2.6
Insurance	2	2.4
Other (e.g., discount/bank brokerage)	44	1.0

Source: Neil Bathon, "2013 Investment Industry Trends Presentation," FUSE Research Network (23 June 2014).

EUROPE AND ASIA

In Europe, retail investment product distribution is fragmented and highly region dependent. In continental Europe, distribution is primarily driven through retail banks (e.g., UniCredit, BNP Paribas) and private banks (e.g., UBS, Credit Suisse), which generally take an "open architecture" approach to offering affiliated and third-party asset management products to investors. The distribution model in the United Kingdom is relatively unique because most products are sold via independent financial advisers (IFAs),[18] who work directly for clients rather than for banks or insurance groups. Retail distribution in Switzerland and in the Nordic countries is driven largely through private banks (e.g., Pictet, SEB).

Although individual Asian mutual fund markets remain relatively small (11% of global mutual fund AUM; see Appendix A) compared with their Western counterparts, growth trends remain attractive to asset managers seeking to tap the wealth of the region's demographic profile and growing middle class. Furthermore, distribution in many Asian markets is dominated by large regional retail banks and global banks with private banking divisions. Asian markets tend to have fractured regulatory regimes with no centralized regulatory system extending across political and geographic borders. Nevertheless, a number of Asian countries continue to work toward a common cross-border regulatory scheme similar to what has developed under the UCITS regime in Europe.

---

[18]IFAs, who must meet a number of strict qualifications, are regulated by the Financial Conduct Authority, the UK's primary financial regulator.

RETAIL PRODUCT PACKAGING

Asset managers primarily package retail investment strategies through CIVs, including mutual funds, UCITS, ETFs, closed-end funds (CEFs),[19] and unit investment trusts (UITs).[20] Collective funds allow asset managers to scale efficiently and to offer such advantages to retail investors as low investment minimums, daily or intraday liquidity, and standardized performance and tax reporting. Additionally, CIVs are generally overseen by trustees with a fiduciary responsibility to shareholders and the authority to hire and/or terminate a fund's investment adviser and service providers.

It is necessary for analysts to be aware of the subscription and redemption mechanics of various investment vehicles in order to properly forecast revenues. For example, open-end mutual funds in the United States allow for daily subscriptions and redemptions and are thus subject to both market-based and investor-driven AUM risk. Alternatively, CEFs are launched via an IPO process and subsequent trading of the fund's shares takes place between investors on market exchanges rather than directly with the fund. As a result, CEFs possess a more predictable revenue stream, setting aside investor-level redemption risk. Some CEFs trading at a persistent discount to NAV have been the target of activist investors seeking to convert the funds to open-end vehicles.

A number of asset managers offer separately managed accounts (SMAs) to wealthy investors. SMAs, which require much higher investment minimums, allow an investor to include/exclude specific holdings and offer more tax flexibility through customized tax gain/loss options. As of March 2013, the retail SMA industry held more than $700 billion in AUM.[21]

RETAIL INVESTOR SEGMENTATION

Retail investors' investment product usage and financial planning services are typically tailored to an individual's needs and are a function of investable financial assets. **Exhibit 6** outlines a general segmentation of investor wealth and product usage.

Targeting high-net-worth investors—those with at least $1 million in investable assets—is a priority for many wealth management firms and asset managers marketing their products through intermediaries. According to the 2014 "World Wealth Report" from Capgemini and RBC Wealth Management, 13.73 million high-net-worth

---

[19]A CEF is an investment company that raises assets through an IPO (and follow-on offerings) and subsequently trades on an exchange. CEF shares are not redeemable by the fund and must be traded on an exchange. The price of a CEF share can trade at, below, or above the fund's NAV based on secondary market demand.
[20]A UIT is an investment company that issues redeemable securities in a public offering. UITs generally invest in a fixed basket of securities for a finite period of time.
[21]Andrew Klausner, "The Death of SMAs (Separately Managed Accounts)?" *Forbes* (12 June 2013): www.forbes.com/sites/advisor/2013/06/12/the-death-of-smas-separately-managed-accounts.

individuals (HNWIs) controlled a record $56.2 trillion in wealth at the end of 2013. Although North America and Asia had approximately equal numbers of HNWIs at the end of 2013, the Asia-Pacific region has witnessed faster growth (see **Table 11**).

Exhibit 6.   Investor Wealth Segments and Product Usage

Investor Segment	Financial Assets	Investment Products
Ultra high net worth	> $30,000,000	▪ Separate accounts ▪ Hedge funds/PE ▪ Mutual funds/UCITS/CEFs ▪ ETFs
High net worth	> $1,000,000	▪ Separate accounts ▪ Hedge funds ▪ Mutual funds/UCITS/CEFs ▪ ETFs
Mass affluent	> $100,000	▪ Mutual funds/UCITS/CEFs
Mass retail	< $100,000	▪ ETFs

Table 11.   HNWI Population by Region, 2008–2013
             (millions)

Region	Year						Percentage Change 2012–2013
	2008	2009	2010	2011	2012	2013	
North America	2.7	3.1	3.4	3.4	3.7	4.3	15.9%
Asia Pacific	2.4	3.0	3.3	3.4	3.7	4.3	17.3
Europe	2.6	3.0	3.1	3.2	3.4	3.8	12.5
Middle East	0.4	0.4	0.4	0.5	0.5	0.6	16.0
Latin America	0.4	0.5	0.5	0.5	0.5	0.5	3.5
Africa	0.1	0.1	0.1	0.1	0.1	0.1	3.7
Total	8.6	10.0	10.9	11.0	12.0	13.7	14.7

Notes: Numbers and quoted percentages may not add up because of rounding. CAGR 2008–2013 = 9.9%.
Source: Capgemini and RBC Wealth Management, "2014 World Wealth Report" (www.capgemini.com/thought-leadership/world-wealth-report-2014-from-capgemini-and-rbc-wealth-management).

INSTITUTIONAL INVESTORS

The realm of institutional investors spans public and private pensions, government/sovereign wealth funds, corporations, insurance companies, and endowments and foundations. Each segment of the institutional market is unique in its goals, asset allocation preferences, and investment strategy needs.

In the United States, it is estimated that more than 80% of institutional investors rely on investment consultants to guide their investment decisions.[22] Investment consultants (e.g., Mercer, Towers Watson) play a key role in advising their institutional clients on investment policy structuring, investment manager selection, asset allocation, asset/liability analysis, and performance monitoring. Increasingly, consultants are acting in a chief investment officer capacity for clients by assuming complete discretionary authority over portfolio decisions. Globally, investment consultants advised on assets estimated at more than $25 trillion as of June 2011.[23] **Table 12** lists the five largest investment consulting firms as of 30 June 2014.

Table 12.   Largest Investment Consulting Firms
($ trillions)

	Assets under Advisement
Mercer	$9.2
Cambridge Associates	4.7
Aon Hewitt Investment Consulting	4.6
Russell Investments	2.6
Towers Watson Investment Services	2.2

Source: Pensions & Investments (www.pionline.com; retrieved 27 December 2014).

---

[22]Amit Goyal and Sunil Wahal, "The Selection and Termination of Investment Management Firms by Plan Sponsors," *Journal of Finance*, vol. 63, no. 4 (August 2008): 1805–1847.

[23]Tim Jenkinson, Howard Jones, and Jose Vicente Martinez, "Picking Winners? Investment Consultants' Recommendations of Fund Managers," working paper (26 September 2014): http://papers.ssrn.com/sol3/papers.cfm?abstract_id=2327042.

PENSION PLANS

Global pension assets approached $32 trillion by the end of 2013. In the United States, public and private defined benefit (DB)[24] pension plans collectively hold approximately $8 trillion in assets and serve as a major source of assets for both traditional and alternative asset managers.[25] The United States represents the largest pension marketplace in the world, comprising more than 58% of global pension assets (see **Table 13**).

Table 13.   Global Pension Assets: 2003, 2013
($ billions)

| | AUM | | |
Market	2003	2013	10-Year CAGR
Australia	$424	$1,565	14.0%
Brazil	83	284	13.1
Canada	636	1,451	8.6
France	139	169	2.0
Germany	229	509	8.3
Hong Kong	37	114	12.1
Ireland	64	130	7.4
Japan	2,906	3,236	1.1
Netherlands	614	1,359	8.3
South Africa	100	236	9.0
Switzerland	355	786	8.3
United Kingdom	1,261	3,263	10.0
United States	9,942	18,878	6.6
Total	$16,787	$31,980	6.7%

Note: US pension assets include DB and DC assets.
Source: Towers Watson, "Global Pension Assets Study 2014" (5 February 2014): www.towerswatson.com/en-US/Insights/IC-Types/Survey-Research-Results/2014/02/Global-Pensions-Asset-Study-2014.

---

[24]Pension plans are typically categorized as either DB or DC. DB plans are employer-sponsored plans that offer employees a fixed, predefined benefit upon retirement. Generally, employers are responsible for the contributions made to the plan and bear the risk associated with adequately funding the benefits offered to employees. DC plans are typically tax-deferred retirement plans funded by both the employee and the employer. Future benefit amounts are unknown and lack any guarantee because the investment risk is assumed by the employee and not by the employer.
[25]Investment Company Institute, "Defined Contribution Plan Participants' Activities, 2013," ICI Research Report (April 2014): www.ici.org/pdf/ppr_13_rec_survey.pdf.

DEFINED BENEFIT

DB plans face a myriad of operational challenges (actuarial, accounting, liquidity, and regulatory) and vary widely in their asset allocation and sophistication, prompting many asset managers to employ dedicated personnel to service this segment of the market.

The long-term outlook for the DB segment is negative: Most pension plan sponsors eschew the complexity, risk, and expense of managing DB plans. Increasingly, DB plan sponsors are closing plans to new employees and freezing retirement benefits for participants.

As shown in **Figure 8**, the general decline in DB plan market share in the United States has been dramatic as plan sponsors have increasingly adopted DC plans. Globally, DC plans represent 47% of pension assets.[26]

Figure 8. **Private Sector Workers Participating in an Employment-Based Retirement Plan, by Plan Type, 1979–2011**

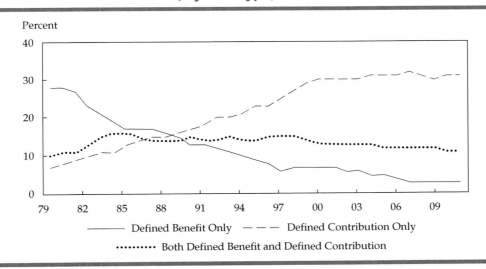

Sources: US Department of Labor Form 5500, Summaries, 1979–1998; Pension Benefit Guaranty Corporation, Current Population Survey, 1999–2011; Employee Benefit Research Institute (EBRI) estimates, 1999–2010 (www.ebri.org/publications/benfaq/index.cfm?fa=retfaqt14fig1).

---

[26]Towers Watson, "Global Pension Assets Study 2014" (5 February 2014): www.towerswatson.com/en-US/Insights/IC-Types/Survey-Research-Results/2014/02/Global-Pensions-Asset-Study-2014.

DEFINED CONTRIBUTION

DC plans represent the dominant form of retirement investing in Australia and the United States, and they are gaining significant momentum in the Netherlands, Canada, and Japan.[27] In the United States, the $5.9 trillion DC market and the $6.5 trillion IRA (individual retirement account) market represent two important sources of assets for managers (see **Table 14**). The "stickiness" of these assets and the continuous contributions made by employees and employers to these accounts over multidecade periods lead to profitable, long-duration AUM for asset managers. According to McKinsey & Company,[28] the average holding period for a mutual fund held in a DC plan is six to seven years, compared with three to four years in a brokerage account.

Table 14.   US Retirement Assets
($ trillions)

Type	Amount
IRAs	$6.5
Federal, state, and local pension plans	5.6
401(k) plans	4.2
Private DB plans	3.0
Annuities	2.0
Other DC plans	1.7

Source: Investment Company Institute, "Defined Contribution Plan Participants' Activities, 2013," ICI Research Report (April 2014): www.ici.org/pdf/ppr_13_rec_survey.pdf.

---

[27]Towers Watson, "Global Pension Assets Study 2014."

[28]McKinsey & Company, "Winning in the Defined Contribution Market of 2015: New Realities Reshape the Competitive Landscape" (http://legacy.plansponsor.com/uploadfiles/mckinseydcreport.pdf; retrieved 27 December 2014).

ENDOWMENTS AND FOUNDATIONS

Endowments and foundations together represent more than $1 trillion in assets.[29] Although smaller than other institutional segments, this channel is attractive because of the long time horizons of endowments and foundations, which are often deemed perpetual. In addition, alternative asset managers benefit from the segment's above-average allocation to alternative and illiquid investment strategies (see **Table 15**). At the end of 2013, the National Association of College and University Business Officers (NACUBO) reported that endowments and foundations held an average 28% allocation to alternative asset classes.[30]

The large allocations to alternative investments are primarily because of the long time horizons of endowments and foundations and the influence of endowment-specific asset allocation models popularized by Yale University's endowment managers David Swensen and Dean Takahashi.[31] **Table 16** outlines the Yale endowment's asset allocation, in which alternative investments represent well over 50% of the portfolio.

Table 15. Asset Allocations for US College and University Endowments and Affiliated Foundations

(FY2013, equal weighted)

Asset Class	Percentage Allocation
Domestic equity	31%
Fixed income	18
Foreign equity	18
Alternatives	28
Cash	5

Source: National Association of College and University Budget Officers and Commonfund Institute, "2013 NACUBO-Commonfund Study of Endowments," NACUBO and Commonfund Institute (2014): www.nacubo.org/Documents/EndowmentFiles/2013NCSEPublicTablesAsset Allocations.pdf.

---

[29]The Foundation Center reports total foundation AUM of $662 billion as of year-end 2011 (http://data.foundationcenter.org/#/foundations/all/nationwide/total/trends:num_foundations/2011). NACUBO reports total endowment AUM of $448.6 billion as of 30 June 2013 (www.nacubo.org/Documents/EndowmentFiles/2013NCSEPressReleaseFinal.pdf).

[30]NACUBO and Commonfund Institute, "2013 NACUBO-Commonfund Study of Endowments," press release (28 January 2014): www.nacubo.org/Documents/EndowmentFiles/2013NCSEPressRelease Final.pdf.

[31]Yale University Investments Office, "The Yale Endowment 2013."

Table 16. Yale Endowment's Asset Allocation
(as of June 2013)

Asset Class	Percentage Allocation
Absolute return	17.8%
Domestic equity	5.9
Fixed income	4.9
Foreign equity	9.8
Natural resources	7.9
PE	32.0
Real estate	20.2
Cash	1.6

Source: Yale University Investments Office, "The Yale Endowment 2013" (http://investments. yale.edu/images/documents/Yale_Endowment_13.pdf; retrieved 27 December 2014).

INSURANCE COMPANIES

As of the end of 2013, insurers held more than $13 trillion in AUM globally, with the United States representing the largest individual market at more than $5.5 trillion. Many insurance companies have in-house portfolio management teams responsible for managing general account assets (i.e., assets available to pay claims and benefits). Moreover, a number of insurers market their portfolio management capabilities to third-party investors, often through separately branded subsidiaries (e.g., MassMutual Financial Group operates several investment management affiliates, including Babson Capital Management and OppenheimerFunds Investment Management). General account portfolio allocations vary among insurer types (life, property and casualty [P&C], reinsurance, fraternal, health, and title) because of the need to appropriately match assets to liabilities as well as unique liquidity and duration considerations (see **Table 17**).[32]

---

[32]For example, life insurers tend to invest in longer-term assets (e.g., 30-year government and corporate bonds) relative to P&C insurers because of the longer-term nature of their liabilities.

Table 17. Insurance Company Asset Allocations
(as of 31 December 2010)

Asset Class	Life	P&C	Health
Cash/short term	3%	7%	18%
Bonds	78	71	60
Equities	1	12	13
Mortgage loans	9	0	0
Other	9	11	9

Source: Davide Serra, "The Insurance Sector: The View from the Outside," The Geneva Association, presentation delivered on 4 November 2014 in London.

Increasingly, insurance companies are choosing to outsource some of their general account portfolio management duties—primarily the management of sophisticated alternative asset classes—to unaffiliated asset managers. In the United States, this trend is especially salient: Outsourced AUM increased 54% over the last four years to more than $2.8 trillion by the end of 2013.[33]

SOVEREIGN WEALTH FUNDS

Sovereign wealth funds (SWFs), state-owned investment funds commonly funded by revenues from commodity exports or from foreign exchange reserves, represent an increasingly attractive segment for asset managers: SWF assets doubled to more than $6.8 trillion from the end of 2007 to 30 September 2014.[34] Unlike DB plans, SWFs typically do not manage specific liability obligations, and they possess a long-term investment horizon with above-average allocations to alternative investments. The majority of assets in SWFs are concentrated in resource-rich countries in Asia and the Middle East. **Table 18** lists the 10 largest SWFs.

Abu Dhabi Investment Authority's broad asset allocation guidelines are provided in **Table 19**. This $773 billion global portfolio spans more than two dozen asset classes and is managed by a number of external asset managers responsible for both passive and active strategies. The majority of the portfolio's equity allocation is passively managed.

---

[33]Randy Diamond, "Insurance Assets Outsourced to Managers Jump 54% in 4 Years," *Pensions & Investments* (1 September 2014): www.pionline.com/article/20140901/PRINT/309019992/insurer-assets-outsourced-to-managers-jump-54-in-4-years.
[34]SWFI, "Sovereign Wealth Fund Rankings."

Table 18. Largest Sovereign Wealth Funds
(as of 30 September 2014, $ billions)

Country	Sovereign Wealth Fund	Assets
Norway	Government Pension Fund—Global	$893
United Arab Emirates (Abu Dhabi)	Abu Dhabi Investment Authority	773
Saudi Arabia	SAMA Foreign Holdings	757
China	China Investment Corporation	653
China	SAFE Investment Company	568
Kuwait	Kuwait Investment Authority	548
China (Hong Kong)	Hong Kong Monetary Authority Investment Portfolio	400
Singapore	Government of Singapore Investment Corporation	320
Qatar	Qatar Investment Authority	256
Singapore	Temasek Holdings	177
Total		$6,800

Source: SWFI, "Sovereign Wealth Fund Rankings" (www.swfinstitute.org/fund-rankings; retrieved 27 December 2014).

Table 19. Abu Dhabi Investment Authority Asset Allocation Guidelines

	Min	Max
Asset class		
Developed equities	32%	42%
Emerging market equities	10	20
Small-cap equities	1	5
Government bonds	10	20
Credit	5	10
Alternative	5	10
Real estate	5	10
PE	2	8
Infrastructure	1	5
Cash	0	10

(continued)

Table 19. Abu Dhabi Investment Authority Asset Allocation Guidelines (continued)

	Min	Max
Region		
North America	35%	50%
Europe	20	35
Developed Asia	10	20
Emerging markets	15	25

Source: Abu Dhabi Investment Authority, "Portfolio Overview" (www.adia.ae/En/Investment/Portfolio.aspx; retrieved 27 December 2014).

MAJOR PRODUCT SEGMENTS

SEPARATELY MANAGED ACCOUNTS

Large institutional investors generally prefer to invest in SMAs. SMAs differ from collective investment funds because the individual securities are purchased in a separate custodial account for the institution and are managed pursuant to a customized investment management agreement (IMA) and a set of specific investment guidelines.

SMAs allow institutional investors to directly own securities and to tailor the asset manager's investment strategy to match the institution's specific portfolio preferences. For example, a public pension plan investing in an asset manager's large value equity strategy might wish to implement a social or public policy stance by excluding any equity ownership of companies engaged in the tobacco business. Also, SMAs afford investors the ability to customize their tax exposures, given that the cost bases of the assets are unique to each investor. Investors generally pursue a number of tax optimization strategies, such as tax-loss harvesting and avoiding short-term capital gains.

SMA vehicles hold a significant share of AUM within the $32 trillion global pension market.[35] In the United States, SMA assets were estimated to be more than $6 trillion as of the end of 2012. A 2014 Securities Industry and Financial Markets Association survey of asset managers that offer separately managed accounts found that half of the institutional investor clients were pension plans (35%) or insurance companies (15%), with the remainder owned by a combination of other official institutions and endowments and foundations.

SMA investor account minimums generally range from $1 million to $100 million, depending on the type of investment strategy (e.g., fixed-income strategies typically require higher minimums to achieve proper diversification) and the asset manager's operational efficiency. Relative to a collective investment vehicle, an SMA, because of its customized nature, generally requires an asset manager to employ more operational and back-office resources.

Institutional investors often negotiate management fee terms when entering into IMAs with asset managers. Large institutional investors that present an attractive revenue opportunity for an asset manager often negotiate favorable fee terms relative to published fee rates. Also, most investors receive scale discounts in the form of a sliding management fee schedule. For example, an institutional investor committing

---

[35]Towers Watson, "Global Pension Assets Study 2014."

$100 million to a small-cap value SMA would be subject to a 0.75% management fee on the first $50 million invested, and any amount more than $50 million would be subject to a 0.65% management fee. In this case, the weighted-average management fee expense to the investor would amount to 0.70%.

MUTUAL FUNDS

Mutual funds represent the primary collective investment vehicle of individual investors globally, with more than $30 trillion in AUM as of the end of 2013.[36] The United States ranks as the largest mutual fund marketplace, with AUM topping $15 trillion by the end of 2013. Mutual fund AUM in the United States represents a high-water mark for the industry, which began in 1924 with the launch of the first mutual fund, Massachusetts Investors Trust, by MFS Investment Management.[37]

Globally, mutual fund markets operate in a similar manner, offering individual investors low investment minimums, diversified portfolios, daily liquidity, and standardized performance and tax reporting. However, the impact of regulations is a function of political and geographical borders. Mutual funds in the United States are legally "open-end"[38] companies, regulated by the SEC and governed by the rules and procedures detailed in the Investment Company Act of 1940 (the 1940 Act). In Europe, the European Union has helped to usher in a collective regulatory framework known as UCITS. UCITS regulation, first introduced in 1985, allows asset managers to distribute funds across all EU member countries, provided that funds are registered with one local country regulator that is a member of the broader European Securities and Markets Authority. UCITS funds are also distributed in jurisdictions outside of the EU, including the Asia-Pacific region, where there are more than 3,500 Luxembourg-domiciled UCITS funds distributed throughout Australia,

---

[36]Investment Company Institute, *2014 Investment Company Fact Book*, 54th ed. (2014), Table 60 (www.icifactbook.org/pdf/14_fb_table60.pdf).

[37]On 16 July 1926, the *Boston Globe* published an article profiling the fund that stated: "The Massachusetts Investors Trust, organized in 1924 to afford the investor an opportunity to purchase a broad list of sound common stocks in convenient units, has grown in the interim from $50,000 paid in to more than $2,500,000 and now numbers just short of 1,000 shareholders. Its funds are invested in the common stocks of 136 leading American corporations. The trustees have acquired the holdings of common stocks for permanent investment, not for speculation. Their selection to date has shown the following interesting results: Of the 136 stocks held, three have passed their dividends, paid extras, or stock dividends or issued results. The result of market fluctuations has been equally favorable. At today's market, 26 of the 136 stocks are selling at less than they cost, but the other 110 issues are selling for enough more so that the value of the trust shares is more than 10 points above the offering price of 52-1/2." "First Mutual Fund (1924)," CelebrateBoston (www.celebrateboston. com/first/mutual-fund.htm; retrieved 27 December 2014).

[38]Open-end funds allow shareholders to purchase and redeem shares of the fund daily at NAV.

Japan, Singapore, and Hong Kong.[39] As of 2013, more than 35,000 UCITS funds were distributed throughout 86 countries.[40]

Overview of US Mutual Fund Regulation: Investment Company Act of 1940

- *Oversight.* A mutual fund must establish a board of trustees or directors who are approved by shareholders. At least 75% of a mutual fund's board must consist of independent directors, and the chairman must be independent.[41]

- *Diversification.* Funds that elect to be labeled "diversified" must meet specific portfolio diversification standards. For example, with respect to 75% of a fund's assets, no more than 5% may be invested in any single investment, and typically, the fund may not own more than 10% of the voting securities of a single company. Funds that elect to be classified as nondiversified follow more liberal portfolio diversification guidelines.

- *Voting rights.* Funds can issue only one class of stock, every share of which must have equal voting rights, although multiple share classes may exist to accommodate different pricing and service offerings.

- *Leverage limitations.* To limit risk, the 1940 Act restricts the use of leverage by limiting borrowing to one-third of a fund's assets.

- *Liquidity.* A fund's illiquid assets must be limited to 15% of the portfolio.

- *Tax treatment.* To qualify as a pass-through tax entity and avoid double taxation, a fund must distribute at least 90% of its interest, dividends, and net realized capital gains earned every year.

---

[39]J.P. Morgan Worldwide Securities Services, "The Future of Asset Management: Exploring New Frontiers," JPMorgan Chase Bank (2010): www.jpmorgan.com/cm/BlobServer/The_Future_of_Asset_Management.pdf?blobkey=id&blobwhere=1320549503851&blobheader=application/pdf&blobheadername1=Cache-Control&blobheadervalue1=private&blobcol=urldata&blobtable=MungoBlobs.

[40]PwC, "Fund Distribution: UCITS and Alternative Investment Funds (AIFs)," PricewaterhouseCoopers (2014): http://download.pwc.com/ie/pubs/2014-pwc-ireland-distribution-knowledge-12-05-2014-1.pdf.

[41]SEC, *Final Rule: Investment Company Governance*, Securities and Exchange Commission (2004): www.sec.gov/rules/final/ic-26520.htm.

Most mutual funds act as "virtual companies" by generally not retaining employees and by outsourcing all aspects of operations (investment management, administration, distribution, etc.) to other companies. These relationships are subject to board approval, often renewable on an annual basis, and are sometimes subject to shareholder approval.

Figure 9 depicts the major relationships between a mutual fund and its shareholders, board, and service providers.

Figure 9. Mutual Fund Major Relationships

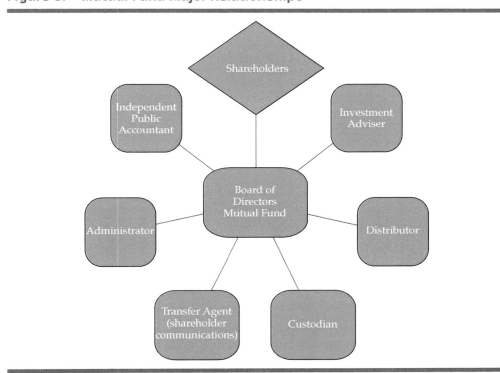

Source: Investment Company Institute, *2014 Investment Company Fact Book*, 54th ed. (2014): www.icifactbook.org/fb_appa.html.

EXCHANGE-TRADED FUNDS

State Street Global Advisors introduced the first ETF in 1993 with the debut of its SPDR S&P 500 (Standard & Poor's Depositary Receipts) on the NYSE. This ETF, designed to track the performance of the world's most popular equity index, the S&P 500, was seeded with $6.5 million in assets and today totals more than $172 billion in AUM, representing one of the most widely traded securities in the world.[42]

ETFs are structured as open-end investment vehicles similar to mutual funds, and in the United States, they are subject to the vast majority of the 1940 Investment Company Act rules. However, investors do not purchase shares of an ETF directly; rather, shares are acquired on secondary market exchanges (e.g., NYSE, NASDAQ). Although ETF share prices closely track a fund's actual NAV,[43] prices can vary based on demand trends among investors, market-making activity from authorized participants, and the underlying liquidity of the securities represented by the ETF.

ETFs have taken hold across investor classes in the institutional and retail marketplaces and represent one of the fastest-growing and most disruptive product categories in the asset management industry. Tactically oriented asset managers value intraday market pricing (mutual funds typically can be purchased or sold only once a day) and the ability to short sell ETFs, whereas long-term investors—both institutional and retail—have increasingly employed ETFs as portfolio building blocks in a diversified asset allocation. ETFs have also benefited from the growing popularity of passive investing in general (see the Industry Trends section).

As of October 2013, the global $2.3 trillion ETF industry included more than 5,000 funds from 215 managers located on 58 exchanges worldwide.[44] (**Table 20** shows global exchange-traded product market share by region.) From 2009 to 2013, assets in ETFs listed in the United States almost doubled from $1.0 trillion to $1.7 trillion, representing a 25.8% CAGR. Although the vast majority of ETFs follow passively managed indexes, a growing number of actively managed ETFs have been introduced by asset managers in recent years. In the United States, actively managed ETFs represented less than 1% of AUM as of year-end 2013, according to FUSE Research Network.

---

[42]State Street Global Advisors, "The First ETF Turns 20: Innovation That Leveled the Playing Field for All Investors Reaches New Milestone," State Street Corporation (29 January 2013): http://newsroom.statestreet.com/press-release/state-street-global-advisors/first-etf-turns-20-innovation-leveled-playing-field-all-i.

[43]NAV refers to a fund's assets minus its liabilities, which typically represent accrued expenses for portfolio management, custody, and other services that are expensed directly to the fund.

[44]EY, "Global ETF Survey: A New Era of Growth and Innovation," EYGM (January 2014): www.ey.com/Publication/vwLUAssets/EY_-_Global_ETF_Survey_2014/$FILE/EY-Global-ETF-Survey-January-2014.pdf.

Table 20. Global Exchange-Traded Product Market Share
(as of 30 September 2014)

Listing Region	AUM ($ billions)	Market Share	No. of Products	AUM/Product
United States	$1,864.3	71%	1,646	1.13
Europe	450.8	17	2,219	0.20
Canada	65.3	2	324	0.20
Latin America	8.5	0	43	0.20
Asia Pacific	186.0	7	694	0.27
Middle East and Africa	45.4	2	377	0.12
Global exchange-traded product industry	2,620.3		5,303	0.49

Source: BlackRock, "ETP Landscape: Industry Highlights," BlackRock Advisors (September 2014): www.blackrockinternational.com/content/groups/internationalsite/documents/literature/etfl_industryhilight_sep14.pdf.

ETF TRANSPARENCY AND ARBITRAGE

Transparency of ETF holdings is essential to helping ETFs track their fair value or NAV. ETFs, whether index tracking or active, are currently required to publish their holdings daily. Only institutional trading firms deemed "authorized participants" (APs) trade directly with an ETF. Authorized participants are usually large institutional trading firms that actively exploit the arbitrage mechanism to profit from any deviation of the ETF's price from its NAV. ETFs typically issue bulk share amounts called "creation units" (typically representing 50,000 shares) to APs in exchange for the underlying securities included in the index that the ETF tracks. This mechanism allows APs to arbitrage any price discrepancy between the ETF's share price as it trades on an exchange and the underlying NAV of the ETF.

The following excerpt from the Investment Company Institute's paper "ETF Basics: The Creation and Redemption Process and Why It Matters" provides a basic overview of the arbitrage APs employ when an ETF's market price deviates from its NAV.

ETF Trades at a Premium to NAV

When an ETF is trading at a premium to its underlying value, authorized participants may sell short the ETF during the day while simultaneously buying the underlying securities. At the end of the day, the authorized participant will deliver the creation basket of securities to the ETF in exchange for ETF shares that they use to cover their short sales. The authorized participant will receive a profit from having paid less for the underlying securities than it received for the ETF shares. The additional supply of ETF shares also should help bring the ETF share price back in line with its underlying value.

ETF Trades at a Discount to NAV

When an ETF is trading at a discount, authorized participants may buy the ETF shares and sell short the underlying securities. At the end of the day, the authorized participant will return ETF shares to the fund in exchange for the ETF's redemption basket of securities, which they will use to cover their short positions. The authorized participant will receive a profit from having paid less for the ETF shares than it received for the underlying security. The lower supply of ETF shares available also should help bring the ETF share price back in line with its underlying value.[45]

The arbitrage pricing mechanism is unique to the ETF vehicle and has resolved a major perceived flaw of CEFs, whose shares are exchange traded and subject to relatively large discounts and premiums to NAV based solely on secondary market demand from investors.

Traditional Asset Manager Case Study: Franklin Resources (Franklin Templeton Investments)

OVERVIEW

Franklin Templeton Investments, based in San Mateo, California, is one of the world's largest and best-known global asset management firms, possessing more than $898 billion in AUM as of 30 September 2014. Founded in 1947, the firm was an early pioneer in investing in overseas markets and today has more than 9,000 employees, of which 600 are investment professionals. Franklin Templeton manages assets for institutional and retail clients located in 150 countries and is regarded as the largest cross-border fund manager. Franklin Templeton is a publicly traded asset manager included in the S&P 500 and listed on the NYSE under the ticker symbol BEN.

---

[45]Mara Shreck and Shelly Antoniewicz, "ETF Basics: The Creation and Redemption Process and Why It Matters," Investment Company Institute (19 January 2012): www.ici.org/viewpoints/view_12_etfbasics_creation.

ASSETS UNDER MANAGEMENT

Franklin Templeton's holdings tend toward traditional asset classes, with 81% of AUM managed in long-only equity and fixed-income assets (see **Table 21**).

Table 21. Franklin Templeton Assets under Management

Investment Category	AUM ($ billions)	Percentage of Total AUM	Notes
Equity	$371.0	41%	Growth, income, value
Hybrid	159.5	18	Asset allocation, flexible, alternatives
Fixed income	361.0	40	Long term, short term
Cash management	7.0	1	Short-term liquidity assets
Total	$898.0	100%	

PRODUCTS MANAGED

Acquisitions have been a major contributor to the growth in Franklin's AUM over the past 60 years. Franklin Templeton's CEO, Greg Johnson, has remarked, "One of the ways that we have built Franklin Templeton's global business is by making strategic investments in smaller, highly experienced asset management companies."[46]

Originally focused on domestic fixed-income and balanced strategies, the Franklin family of funds has expanded over the decades across the capital spectrum. The firm began to diversify into alternative investments with the purchase of hedge fund specialist K2 Advisors.

Exhibit 7 provides a summary of key acquisitions and investments made by Franklin.

Exhibit 7. Franklin Templeton Acquisition Timeline

Year	Capability Added	Target
Domestic		
1992	■ Global equities ■ Value equities	■ Templeton, Galbraith & Hansberger
1996	■ Value equities	■ Heine Securities/Mutual Series Fund
2012	■ Hedge fund of funds	■ K2 Advisors LLC

(continued)

[46]Franklin Templeton Investments, "Franklin Templeton Announces Agreement to Acquire Majority Stake in Fund of Hedge Funds Specialist K2 Advisors," press release, Franklin Resources (19 September 2012): http://phx.corporate-ir.net/phoenix.zhtml?c=111222&p=irol-newsArticle_print&ID=1736473.

Exhibit 7. Franklin Templeton Acquisition Timeline (continued)

Year	Capability Added	Target
International		
2000	■ Korean	■ Ssangyong Templeton Investment Trust Management
2000	■ Canadian fixed income ■ Growth equities	■ Bissett & Associates
2002	■ Indian equities	■ Pioneer ITI AMC
2003	■ Emerging markets PE	■ Darby
2006	■ Brazilian equity and fixed income	■ Bradesco
2011	■ UK equities	■ Rensburg
2011	■ Australian equities	■ Balanced Equity Management

OVERSEAS REACH

Many asset managers strive to create a globally diversified business to spread risk across regions, client types, and asset classes. Specifically, overseas markets offer asset managers a ripe opportunity to manage the wealth of the growing middle class, given that an estimated 80% of the global middle class will be located in developing countries by 2030. That said, Franklin Templeton represents a leading example of a domestic asset manager that has successfully built a global investment and sales platform. The firm's 9,000 employees are located in 35 countries and serve clients in more than 150 countries. International investments represent 35% of total AUM, and in fiscal year 2013, more than half of long-term (i.e., not money market) investment product sales occurred outside the United States. Franklin is also regarded as possessing the largest individual retail cross-border fund umbrella in the world.

Source: Franklin Resources, "Annual Report 2013" (https://materials.proxyvote.com/Approved/354613/20140114/AR_190616; retrieved 28 December 2014).

DEFINED CONTRIBUTION/TARGET-DATE FUND GROWTH

In the wake of several high-profile pension failures and a deep shortfall in the federally guaranteed pension insurance backstop, the Pension Protection Act (PPA) was enacted in 2006. Some view the PPA as the most important retirement legislation enacted in the United States since the Employee Retirement Income Security Act was passed in 1974. While providing a number of reforms to DB plans, the PPA also included a number of provisions that have benefited the DC market. Specifically, the PPA provided statutory authority to allow employers to automatically enroll employees in DC plans. In addition to auto-enrollment, the PPA established Qualified Default Investment Alternatives (QDIAs) to protect employers from potential liabilities arising from losses linked to investments made by automatically enrolled employees. Auto-enrollment is an important catalyst for growth for the DC market and for providers of investment strategies that qualify as QDIA options, such as target-date mutual funds.

Target-date funds are designed to provide an investor with a complete diversified portfolio of asset class exposures, ranging from global equities to fixed-income securities, that automatically rebalances and shifts asset allocation exposures over time to a more conservative posture as the fund reaches a predefined target date (e.g., 2060) meant to coincide with an investor's estimated retirement date. Target-date funds often take the form of funds of funds and are primarily offered by managers with large affiliated retirement recordkeeping platforms that service the operational requirements of DC plan sponsors.

The ease and legal protections provided by the PPA have spurred widespread inclusion of target-date funds within DC plans. An Employee Benefit Research Institute/Investment Company Institute study estimated that the number of investors (plan participants) in target-date funds increased from 19% in 2006 to 41% by the end of 2012. **Table 22** demonstrates the dramatic growth in target-date mutual fund assets over time.

Table 22.   Target-Date Mutual Fund Assets under Management
($ billions)

Year	AUM
2005	$71
2006	115
2007	183
2008	160
2009	256
2010	340
2011	376
2012	481
2013	618

Note: Eight-year AUM CAGR: Target-date funds = 31%; overall fund industry = 7%.
Source: Investment Company Institute, *2014 Investment Company Fact Book.*

RISE OF PASSIVE INVESTING

Institutions and individual investors continue to allocate an increasing percentage of their investments to passively managed investment strategies. The motivation behind this trend is largely attributable to expense savings and the difficulty investors face when attempting to select an asset manager that will provide *ex ante* alpha.

- *Expense savings.* Relative to an actively managed strategy, an index strategy can be accomplished with limited personnel dedicated to maintaining the proper index constituents and processing corporate actions (mergers and acquisitions, spinoffs). Today, retail investors can obtain exposure to the Dow Jones US Large-Cap Total Stock Market Index for as little as 4 bps,[47] whereas large institutional investors can obtain exposure for even less through a separately managed account.

  The average turnover of an index strategy is generally a fraction of the average for an actively managed strategy. Lower portfolio turnover typically leads

---

[47]Charles Schwab, "Schwab ETFs" (www.csimfunds.com/public/csim/home/products/product_finder?producttype=etf; retrieved 28 December 2014).

to lower trading commissions and higher tax efficiency because fewer gains are triggered.

■ *Underperformance.* Persistent underperformance of the average active manager continues to influence investors to pursue index-based investment strategies, especially in the most information-efficient markets, such as large-cap stocks. The S&P Indices Versus Active (SPIVA) report regularly measures the performance of active managers against relevant S&P benchmarks. The 2013 SPIVA US Scorecard found that the majority of active managers across all domestic equity investment categories underperformed their respective benchmarks over the trailing three- and five-year periods.[48]

Table 23 breaks out mutual fund industry assets into actively and passively managed strategies. Nearly two-thirds of investors index "large blend," which is consistent with the trend of investors indexing the most efficient areas of the market.

Table 23. Active vs. Passive, Historical AUM Growth
(\$ trillions, includes US mutual funds and ETFs)

Year	Passive	Active	Total
2003	\$0.6	\$4.3	\$4.9
2004	0.8	5.0	5.7
2005	0.9	5.5	6.4
2006	1.2	6.4	7.6
2007	1.6	7.1	8.6
2008	1.2	4.5	5.7
2009	1.7	6.1	7.8
2010	2.1	7.0	9.1
2011	2.2	6.9	9.1
2012	2.7	7.9	10.7
2013	3.6	9.3	12.8

Note: Ten-year CAGR: overall = 10%, active = 8%, passive = 20%.
Source: FUSE Research Network.

---

[48]S&P Dow Jones Indices, "S&P Indices versus Active Funds (SPIVA) U.S. Scorecard," McGraw Hill Financial (2014): http://us.spindices.com/documents/spiva/spiva-us-year-end-2013.pdf?force_download=true.

GROWTH OF ALTERNATIVE INVESTING

The 2008 financial crisis and ensuing recession called institutional and retail investors' attention to the importance of managing risk. The decline in value of almost all risk assets helped underscore the short-term failings of traditional asset allocation models. A byproduct of 2008's market drawdown was an increased demand for noncorrelated asset classes to serve as ballast in an investor's asset allocation. In the second quarter of 2014, the global hedge fund industry's AUM hit an all-time peak of $2.3 trillion (see **Table 24**).

Although hedge fund usage has always been prevalent among institutional investors, retail investors have increasingly been incorporating hedge fund strategies (packaged through collective investment vehicles, such as mutual funds and UCITS) into their portfolios. The "downstreaming" of hedge fund strategies to retail investors has been especially prevalent in the United States, where, since 2009, more than $130 billion in net new dollars has been allocated to mutual funds categorized as alternative. Alternative AUM in the mutual fund space have grown at a 40% CAGR over the last five years, compared with 6% for the overall US fund industry. A survey

Table 24.   **Hedge Fund Industry AUM**
         ($ trillions)

Year	Amount
2002	$0.5
2003	0.8
2004	1.2
2005	1.4
2006	1.7
2007	2.1
2008	1.5
2009	1.6
2010	1.7
2011	1.7
2012	1.8
2013	2.2
2Q 2014	2.4

Source: BarclayHedge, "Hedge Fund Industry" (www.barclayhedge.com/research/indices/ghs/mum/Hedge_Fund.html; retrieved 28 December 2014).

of US financial advisers demonstrates that much of the growth in alternatives has been associated with reducing portfolio risk through the use of uncorrelated alternative strategies (see **Figure 10**).

Table 25 provides an overview of the growing presence of alternative strategies in the mutual fund industry in the United States.

PricewaterhouseCoopers (PwC) projects that global alternative AUM (defined broadly as hedge funds, PE, etc.) will reach $13 trillion by 2020, representing 13% of global AUM (see **Figure 11**).

Figure 10.   Why Do Advisers Utilize Alternatives?

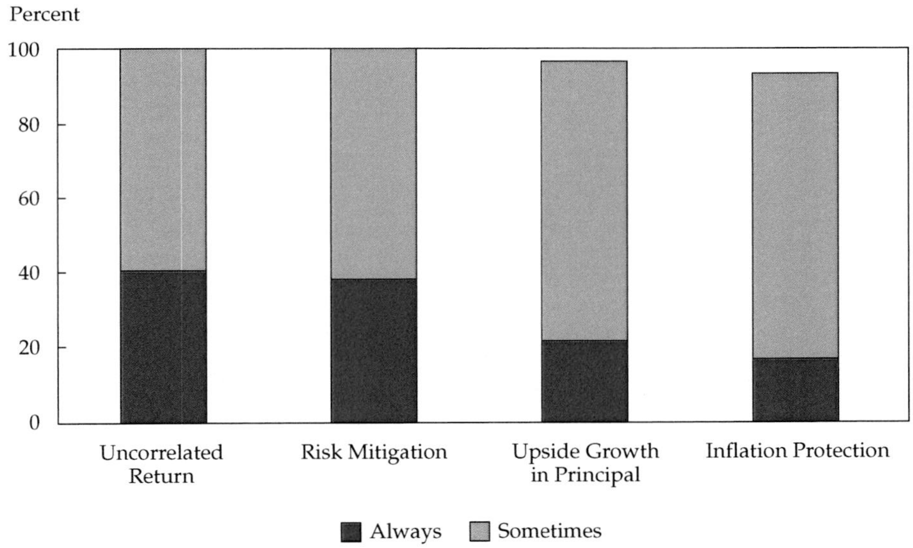

Source: FUSE Research Network.

Table 25. US Alternative Mutual Fund Assets and Net Flows by Strategy
($ millions)

	AUM				Net Flows				
Category	2008	2013	5-Year CAGR	Market Share	2009	2010	2011	2012	2013
Absolute return	$6,166	$70,656	63%	40%	$3,626	$12,301	$874	$9,300	$31,330
Multistrategy	4,072	29,040	48	16	1,736	4,823	4,224	4,255	6,707
Equity long–short	4,909	21,508	34	12	1,165	1,947	2,117	2,704	7,079
Risk-managed equity	9,599	15,808	10	9	1,798	1,761	308	1,232	(419)
Arbitrage	1,652	13,443	52	8	1,770	4,171	2,662	562	1,653
Managed futures	1,439	11,892	53	7	1,449	2,209	6,677	308	1,395
Market neutral	5,725	10,000	12	6	2,137	198	(469)	(380)	1,870
Credit long–short	14	5,378	230	3	61	227	228	731	3,915
Total	$33,576	$177,725	40%		$13,742	$27,636	$16,623	$18,713	$53,530

Source: FUSE Research Network.

Figure 11. Global Alternative AUM Projection

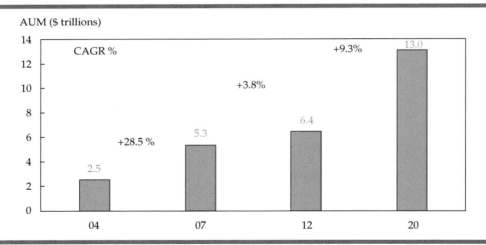

AUM ($ trillions)

Source: PwC, "Asset Management 2020: A Brave New World," PwC (2014): www.pwc.com/gx/en/asset-management/publications/asset-management-2020-a-brave-new-world.jhtml; retrieved 28 December 2014.

ANALYZING ASSET MANAGEMENT COMPANIES

OWNERSHIP STRUCTURE

The ownership structure of investment managers varies, although the vast majority of advisers are privately owned. Ownership structure can play an important role in retaining and incentivizing key personnel, and it is often a metric examined by professional investment consultants when assessing the alignment between asset managers and investors; owners who are portfolio managers with personal capital invested in their strategies are viewed favorably. Ownership stakes are routinely offered to key investment and management professionals as a long-term retention incentive.

PRIVATE CORPORATIONS

The vast majority of investment adviser firms are privately owned by individuals who were original founders or who play key roles in the firm's management. These firms are typically structured as limited liability companies or limited partnerships. In addition, PE firms (e.g., TA Associates, Crestview Partners, Lightyear, ORIX) and asset management holding companies (e.g., AMG, Old Mutual Asset Managers)[49] often take a stake in privately owned asset management firms and assist in management buyouts.

PUBLICLY TRADED

By the end of 2013, there were approximately two dozen pure-play publicly traded asset managers listed on US exchanges. A number of publicly traded diversified financial services (e.g., BNY Mellon, State Street) also possess significant asset management divisions that represent reportable business segments. Globally, approximately 30 significant pure-play asset managers trade publicly, with higher concentrations in Australia, Canada, and the United Kingdom.

---

[49]AMG (ticker symbol: AMG) and Old Mutual Asset Managers (ticker symbol: OMAM) are both publicly traded on the NYSE.

SHAREHOLDER OWNED

The Vanguard Group's ownership is unique because it is the only client-owned mutual fund company. Normally, a mutual fund manager is owned by third-party shareholders (public or private) and manages a series of funds that, in turn, are owned by the shareholders. However, Vanguard's fund shareholders own the firm's mutual funds, which, in turn, own Vanguard (i.e., Vanguard is a "mutual" mutual company).[50] Vanguard's vast scale and ability to operate "at cost" has served as a major competitive advantage, allowing it to offer substantially lower-cost investment products—both actively and passively managed—relative to most competitors.

BARRIERS TO ENTRY

Thousands of asset managers operate in today's highly competitive global asset management industry. Although new entrants into the market don't initially face onerous business hurdles, competing with the largest asset managers has become increasingly difficult.

INVESTMENT TRACK RECORDS

Possessing a consistent track record of peer- and benchmark-beating performance represents the single most important attribute for a manager seeking to attract client assets. Managers must often possess at least a three-year investment track record to even qualify for most investment manager searches. In the venture capital and buy-out spaces, where firms compete aggressively for deals, the top-performing managers often garner "first looks" at the most attractive deals because of their reputation among entrepreneurs and management teams. That said, startup managers backed by established portfolio managers are often able to attract client assets based on attractive track records built at previous firms.

PRODUCT DIFFERENTIATION

Continually offering compelling investment products to fulfill investor demand and meet the needs of varying macroeconomic environments is an essential task for asset managers and requires extensive firm resources. In addition, investors are increasingly seeking customized solutions and have been granting more discretionary latitude to asset managers in order to pursue multi-asset and global investment strategies. In order to effectively offer these solution-oriented products, managers

---

[50]Vanguard Group, "Why Ownership Matters" (https://about.vanguard.com/what-sets-vanguard-apart/why-ownership-matters; retrieved 28 December 2014).

must possess a credible global investment platform coupled with a deep legal, compliance, and marketing infrastructure.

ECONOMIES OF SCALE

Large asset managers often use their scale to negotiate favorable contract terms across divisions, including compliance, technology, operations, and distribution. National distribution firms (e.g., brokerages) tend to grant preferential access to large asset management firms with sales and marketing staff that can adequately service their distribution networks. Furthermore, many retail-oriented distributors often establish revenue-sharing agreements with asset managers seeking to distribute products through their platforms. The prevalence of revenue sharing between asset managers and distributors varies greatly across markets.

DISTRIBUTION AND BRAND REACH

Asset managers with long operating histories often possess diverse institutional and retail distribution relationships with wealth management firms and investment consultants. Cementing relationships with distributors and consultants is often an expensive multiyear effort. Distributors selling investment products to retail investors tend to prefer established and recognized brands from asset managers with long operating histories. Many asset managers that are part of a broader financial services organization have access to large affiliated distribution outlets (e.g., bank branches, insurance representatives) through which products can be sold on a preferred basis.

REGULATION AND COMPLIANCE

The costs of complying with government and self-regulatory organization regulations increased markedly in the wake of the 2008 financial crisis. The additional fixed costs linked to complying with new regulations have been especially burdensome to smaller asset managers. Two recent regulatory developments are highlighted as follows:

- *AIFMD.* The Alternative Investment Fund Managers Directive, issued by the EU in 2013, is expected to have a material impact on the future evolution of the alternative investment business in Europe. The new rules harmonize regulation across the region and are expected to add significant incremental legal and compliance costs for managers. Moreover, the directive adds a number of controversial requirements related to compensation for senior management and portfolio managers.

- *Risk retention rules.* In the United States, several regulators, including the Federal Deposit Insurance Corporation, the Office of the Comptroller of the Currency, and the Federal Housing Finance Agency, implemented rules requiring structured securities managers (e.g., collateralized loan obligation managers) to retain a 5% interest in the securities they issue. This capital commitment, which is designed to encourage managers to have "skin in the game," is expected to be onerous for smaller asset managers with limited balance sheet capital to deploy. Similar risk retention requirements have already been introduced in Europe.

FINANCIAL STATEMENT ANALYSIS

ASSET MANAGER FINANCIALS

The asset management industry is a "professional services" business that requires little physical capital and relies heavily on human capital inputs. These human inputs often constitute the majority of an asset manager's expense base, inclusive of salaries, benefits, incentive compensation (cash, deferred compensation, equity), and commissions, which are typically a percentage (measured in basis points) paid on gross sales of investment products by distribution personnel. Operations and technology-related spending (e.g., fund accounting systems, portfolio management systems, Bloomberg terminals) often make up the remainder of the expense base.

The balance sheets of most asset managers are straightforward, and most publicly traded asset managers carrying public debt possess investment-grade ratings (with the exception of PE-backed managers, which often take on significant debt within their capital structure).

In aggregate, traditional asset manager revenues are largely derived from recurring management fees or "base" fees, supplemented by performance fees and distribution and/or service fees. Of course, alternative-focused managers (hedge funds and PE firms) rely heavily on performance fee and/or carried interest revenue, which can often represent a multiple of management fee revenue. In general, the asset management industry has traditionally been characterized by its embedded operating leverage, which has resulted in high margins relative to other financial and nonfinancial industries. As AUM increase—actively via organic growth (i.e., net new sales) and investment alpha (i.e., portfolio management's contribution to AUM growth outside of beta returns) and passively through market appreciation—the compounding effect of management and performance fees can be a compelling driver of higher margins.

Margins in the industry tend to be fairly resilient given the ability of asset managers to adapt to deteriorating market and business environments. Low capital expenditure requirements and the cost flexibility embedded in most managers' profit and loss accounts allow a manager to translate earnings into strong cash flow. On average, 50%–60% of most asset managers' expenses are discretionary in nature (e.g., discretionary compensation, marketing, travel and entertainment) or vary directly with revenue (e.g., commissions paid to distribution personnel on new sales). On average, public asset managers achieve pretax operating margins in the mid- to low-30% range, whereas the top quartile of managers (usually focused on higher-fee-earning equities and alternatives) regularly produce margins in the 40%–50% range.

The 2008 financial crisis and the effects felt in 2009 tested the resiliency of asset managers' operating models. Asset manager operating margins, which are most sensitive to levels of AUM, experienced material declines of approximately 5%–8% from peak 2007 margins, which were typically in the 35%–40% range (see **Table 26**). Almost universally, managers displayed their margin resiliency through discretionary spending cuts and/or head count reductions. The extent of expense cuts varied widely by asset and ownership structure. Publicly owned asset managers felt investor pressure, whereas managers that were subsidiaries of large banking or insurance groups were relied on to deliver solid margins amid turmoil in their core operating businesses.

Table 26. Operating Margins as a Share of Net Revenues (bps)

Year	Margin
2008	37
2009	32
2010	36
2011	36
2012	37
2013	39

Note: Net revenues are defined as management fee revenues minus distribution costs.
Source: Shub, et al., "Global Asset Management 2014: Steering the Course to Growth."

MANAGEMENT FEE REVENUE

Management or investment advisory fee revenue often represents the largest component of an asset manager's total revenues, especially within the traditional asset manager universe. Management fees are generally calculated as a fixed percentage of the fair value of net AUM (see **Table 27**). AUM is primarily influenced by capital market appreciation/depreciation and net flows (the net effect of client purchases and redemptions). Industrywide, management fees are generally billed either monthly or quarterly and are accounted for on an accrual basis.

Table 27. US Industry Asset-Weighted Average Management Fee Rates (bps)

	Industry Average		
For Fiscal Years Ended 30 September	2013	2012	2011
Equity			
Global/international	60	61	63
United States	44	45	47
Hybrid	39	39	40
Fixed income			
Tax free	36	37	37
Taxable			
Global/international	57	58	56
United States	38	37	38
Cash management	13	13	16

Notes: "U.S. industry asset-weighted average management fee rates were calculated using information available from Lipper® Inc. as of 30 September 2013, 2012, and 2011 and include all U.S.-registered open-end funds that reported expense data to Lipper Inc. as of the funds' most recent annual report date, and for which expenses were equal to or greater than zero. As defined by Lipper Inc., management fees include fees from providing advisory and fund administration services. The averages combine retail and institutional funds data and include all share classes and distribution channels, without exception. Variable annuity products are not included."

Source: Franklin Resources, "Annual Report 2013," Franklin Templeton Investments (https://materials.proxyvote.com/Approved/354613/20140114/AR_190616; retrieved 28 December 2014).

For alternative asset managers, management fees generally cover overhead expenses, but they can generate significant profit depending on a manager's scale. Hedge fund management fees for single-manager strategies average 172 bps in North America.[51]

For PE managers, management fees are typically earned on capital commitments during the investment period and on invested capital at cost. The management fees can range from 1% to 2% and may be reduced following a fund's investment period.

---

[51]Preqin, "Hedge Funds: The Fee Debate; An End to '2 & 20'?," Preqin Research Report (April 2010): www.preqin.com/docs/reports/Preqin_HF_T&C_april_2010.pdf.

Management fees are generally collected directly from funds; accounts receivable issues are, therefore, relatively benign in the asset management business as compared with other industries.

PERFORMANCE FEES

Alternative asset managers and some traditional managers collect performance fees, which are contingent fees charged in addition to management fees. Performance fees are generally calculated in one of two ways: as a percentage of absolute investment results or as a percentage of investment results in excess of a stated benchmark over a stipulated period of time. Performance fees usually range from 10% to 20% of profits, and they are often used by investment managers to pay the portfolio management team's incentive compensation (typically a 40%–50% payout).

Performance fees for hedge funds are often linked to high-water mark provisions that are perpetual in nature but may be reset after a defined period. High-water marks generally ensure that if a strategy underperforms relative to its performance bogey—an absolute return goal or a relative one versus a benchmark—it must gain back any underperformance before any future performance-based fees can be collected. A high-water mark is an investor-friendly provision that prevents an asset manager from collecting performance fees on the same investment gains more than once. Also, many funds include "hurdles," which set a minimum return level that must be achieved before a performance fee can be collected (e.g., LIBOR plus 3%).

> **Performance Fee Calculation**
>
> Consider an investment of $100 million in a hedge fund charging a 20% performance fee. If the fund's NAV increased 20%, the investment would be worth $120 million. Of the $20 million gain, 20%, or $4 million, would be earned by the hedge fund manager, reducing the fund's NAV and the investment to $116 million, representing a 16% gain before any other expense deductions (management fees, administrative expenses, etc.). If the fund included a hurdle of 10%, the performance fee would apply only to the additional 10% gain above and beyond the hurdle rate.

Analysts often examine the percentage of a manager's AUM subject to performance fees to determine the relative impact performance fees have on overall revenue. This metric can be further expanded by examining the percentage of assets subject to performance fees that are above their respective high-water marks to help determine how influential a manager's potential performance-based fee revenue will be in the overall revenue story. It is important to note that asset managers typically accrue performance fee revenues on an "as if" basis, meaning that a fund that is outperforming its benchmark (or other relevant measure) will record performance fee revenue whether or not such amounts have been collected (most hedge funds typically pay out, or "crystallize," once a year). Therefore, it is essential to focus on the cash earnings of alternative managers because performance accruals can reverse over the course of the year if the fund experiences underperformance.[52] (Carried interest terms and clawbacks are discussed previously in the Private Equity and Venture Capital section.)

INVESTMENT INCOME

PE managers often invest alongside limited partners and generate principal gains (or losses) from investments in funds.

It's important to note that under US GAAP, financial statements for alternative managers (and many traditional managers) contain the results of funds and other private investment vehicles (typically PE funds and structured vehicles) that are required to be consolidated because of related party and control issues. The inclusion of the consolidated funds distorts the true underlying operating performance of the asset manager.[53] Asset managers provide a wide variety of non-GAAP reporting and metrics to assist in the evaluation of the underlying operations, but these non-GAAP measures can vary widely.

ADMINISTRATIVE REVENUE

A number of operational and shareholder-related services, such as fund accounting, fund administration, and transfer agency (shareholder call centers), are often provided by asset managers in-house and can represent a material source of earnings. Revenue derived from these services is often tied to a percentage of AUM or to transaction volume.

---

[52]In the United States, alternative asset managers don't incur negative realized performance fees. Their performance fees are asymmetrical and can be either zero or positive. However, within the US mutual fund space, performance fees must be structured symmetrically. It is essential to closely follow accounting guidelines regarding the recognition of performance fees and carried interest revenue because these guidelines continue to evolve across jurisdictions.

[53]A valuable discussion on the fundamentals of PE financials is provided in the Carlyle Group's publication "Understanding Carlyle's Financial Statements" (April 2012): http://files.shareholder.com/downloads/AMDA-UYH8V/0x0x578284/78a9d61e-4760-4c5e-80df-0aa883f15c4d/2012_Carlyle%20Financial%20Statements.pdf.

BUSINESS METRICS

Asset manager success is usually defined by a common set of metrics, including investment performance, distribution prowess, and brand strength. Achieving success across these metrics is key to increasing AUM. However, general capital market risk represents a significant variable outside the control of asset managers. To help mitigate market risk, many asset managers pursue a strategy of diversifying their overall asset mix to achieve a balance of equity and fixed-income assets across geographies. Moreover, many asset managers aim to diversify their underlying client bases among retail and institutional investors. Increasingly, pursuing a global client base represents a core strategic goal of large US asset managers.

ASSETS UNDER MANAGEMENT

Numerous regulatory definitions of AUM exist; however, the term generally refers to the fair market value of assets subject to the firm's discretion and management fees. AUM is the most widely used metric to discern the size and scale of an asset manager; additional metrics include general market movements, net client flows (gross sales less gross redemptions), currency movements, and acquisition activity. **Table 28** shows changes in BlackRock's AUM over the five years ending with 2013.

Table 28. BlackRock AUM, Component Changes by Product Type
($ millions)

	Component Changes in AUM by Product Type, Five Years Ended 31 December 2013					
	31 Dec 2008	Net New Business	Acquired AUM Net	Market/ Foreign Exchange	31 Dec 2013	Five-Year CAGR
Equity	$203,292	$260,503	$1,061,801	$792,099	$2,317,695	63%
Fixed income	481,365	17,779	502,988	240,054	1,242,186	21
Multi-asset	77,516	139,077	45,907	78,714	341,214	35
Alternatives	61,544	(19,722)	68,351	941	111,114	13
Long term	823,717	397,637	1,679,047	1,111,808	4,012,209	37
Cash management	338,439	(118,341)	53,616	1,840	275,554	(4)
Advisory	144,995	(112,263)	(10)	3,603	36,325	(24)
Total	$1,307,151	$167,033	$1,732,653	$1,117,251	$4,324,088	27%

Source: BlackRock, "2013 Annual Report" (www.blackrock.com/corporate/en-us/investor-relations; retrieved 28 December 2014).

However, not all AUM are created equal. Generally, AUM sourced from institutions are considered "stickier" because the frictional costs to clients of switching separately managed account mandates are higher than those for retail investors trading out of collective investment vehicles with daily subscription/redemption features. Additionally, institutional investors often pursue a lengthy committee approach to making asset manager hiring and firing decisions.

Understanding an asset manager's asset class mix is essential. Diversifying an asset mix across the capital spectrum generally helps to reduce revenue volatility caused by market movements. Also, asset managers with deep product offerings can shift their sales and marketing resources to products currently in favor in an effort to generate organic growth and offset redemptions from out-of-favor asset classes. In today's low-rate environment, asset managers with significant money market fund assets have suffered because they have been waiving management fees to support a stable $1 per share NAV.

Assessing a manager's weighted fee rate trends (Investment management fee revenue/Average AUM) alerts an analyst to shifts in a manager's underlying asset base and is especially useful on a time-series basis. This metric can be influenced by capital market trends and/or organic flow (both sales and redemptions). It is important to examine average AUM at a point in time because period-ending AUM can present a mismatch between AUM and earnings.

MARKET APPRECIATION/DEPRECIATION

Capital market movements substantially influence a firm's AUM, and understanding a manager's underlying asset class exposure is essential. Market movements can have a material impact on an asset manager's AUM and thus its revenue. However, given the tendency of capital markets to achieve positive returns over time, asset managers generally benefit from the tailwind of positive long-term market movements.

SALES AND REDEMPTIONS

Gross sales and redemptions measure the inflow and outflow, respectively, of client assets to and from an asset manager's investment strategies. The net effect of sales and redemptions is a number referred to as "net inflows" when positive and "net outflows" when negative. Growth from net inflows is described as "organic growth," and it is often divided by the beginning period AUM to calculate an organic growth rate. A firm with $100 billion in AUM as of year-end 2013 that saw $5 billion in net sales in the first quarter of 2014 would have achieved a 20% annualized organic growth rate.

REDEMPTION RATE

Retention of client assets is critical to an asset manager's profitability, given that many asset managers pay their distribution staff upfront commissions based on gross sales. The redemption rate seeks to measure the "stickiness" of AUM by dividing current period sales by prior period-ending AUM. For example, if a manager's 2012 year-end AUM was $9 billion and 2013 redemptions through 30 June were $3 billion, the redemption rate would be calculated as $3 billion/$9 billion, or 33%, implying that assets were turning over every three years (average AUM over the designated period can be used as well). Unlike open-end funds, CEFs (e.g., PE structures) typically do not permit redemptions of capital prior to the end of a fund's specified term.

INVESTMENT PERFORMANCE

It is often noted that the asset management business is a "relative game" because asset managers are judged by their performance relative to their benchmarks and their peers. To determine the breadth of value (i.e., alpha) that asset managers are adding, analysts often calculate and compare the percentage of investment strategies that are outperforming their respective benchmarks and peers (via category rankings). Investors and consultants typically analyze over multiple time periods, with longer time periods (generally 3–5 years and 10 years) receiving the most attention. In addition, rolling investment returns over multiple market cycles should be examined to determine the consistency of returns over time and to mitigate the risk of endpoint biases.

Morningstar ratings are a highly influential performance metric within the US mutual fund industry and should be closely followed by traditional asset managers who have significant mutual fund assets. The ratings, which range from one (worst) to five (best) stars, are based on a risk-adjusted return measure that rewards funds for consistent performance with less relative downside volatility. The top 10% of funds in each Morningstar category receive five stars; the next 22.5% receive four stars; the next 35%, three stars; the next 22.5%, two stars; and the bottom 10%, one star. Four- and five-star-rated mutual funds have historically captured the vast share of industry net flows despite the questionable predictive power of the ratings.[54] (Performance is further discussed in the Major Risks section.)

---

[54]Christopher B. Philips and Francis M. Kinniry, Jr., "Mutual Fund Ratings and Future Performance," Vanguard Group (June 2010): www.vanguard.com/pdf/icrwmf.pdf.

INVESTMENT CAPACITY

In smaller asset class segments, asset managers are constrained in their ability to grow assets under management indefinitely in certain strategies (e.g., small-cap stocks) because of the inverse relationship that often exists between AUM and investment performance.

Capacity limits, therefore, can act as a governor on revenue potential; as assets approach capacity thresholds, asset managers refuse new accounts to limit AUM growth. Understanding an asset manager's capacity limits is crucial in determining forward earnings, and these limits will often prompt asset managers to deploy capital to develop new capabilities, either organically or through acquisitions. (See **Table 29** for recent merger and acquisition statistics.)

Table 29. Global Merger and Acquisition Activity
($ billions)

	US Based		Ex-United States	
	Aggregate Transaction Value	Number of Transactions	Aggregate Transaction Value	Number of Transactions
2010	$4.8	84	$13.4	96
2011	5.4	88	11.9	93
2012	7.7	88	11.2	91
2013	5.6	78	16.6	110

Source: John H. Temple, David W. Abbott, and Richard H. Haywood, Jr., "The Cambridge Commentary: A Review of Developments in the Investment Management Industry during 2013," Cambridge International Partners (January 2014): www.cambintl.com/Customer-Content/WWW/CMS/files/Cambridge_Commentary_2013.pdf.

VALUATION METRICS

Valuation of asset managers typically involves discounted cash flow (DCF) analysis combined with the use of market multiples. DCF models rely on a number of key assumptions, including the following:

- Market returns

- Net flows (gross sales minus gross redemptions) and fundraising efforts

- Operating margins

- Investment fee rates (Revenue/Average AUM)

- Market multiples

- Net share buybacks

- Recurring versus performance fees

- Cash versus accrued earnings (cash earnings are critical for alternative managers)

- Stage of capital market cycle and PE cycle (diversity of funds in different stages of fundraising, investing, and exiting)

When using market-based metrics, it is important to note that the publicly traded investment management universe is limited to approximately two dozen firms and most public managers fall within the "traditional" categorization, earning most of their revenue from management fees. Because management fee revenues are "recurring" and more predictable, the market tends to place a higher multiple on earnings from traditional asset managers relative to alternative managers, which tend to rely on lumpy performance fee revenue. In addition, many alternative managers in the United States are structured as partnerships, as opposed to corporations, and thus have favorable tax treatment. Some analysts view this structure as untenable and conservatively input full tax rates in their models. (**Table 30** presents valuation metrics for a number of asset managers.)

Table 30. Asset Managers by Geography, Valuation Metrics

	Market Capitalization ($ billions)			Enterprise Value/ LTM EBITDA			Price/AUM (bps)			Price/ LTM Earnings		
	Mar/13	Dec/13	Mar/14	Mar/13	Dec/13	Mar/14	Mar/13	Dec/13	Mar/14	Mar/13	Dec/13	Mar/14
United States												
Affiliated Managers Group	$8.3	$11.5	$10.7	14.6	14.6	12.1	1.5	2.1	1.9	46.8	42.5	30.6
Apollo Global Management	2.9	4.5	4.7	NA	NA	NA	NA	NA	NA	10.5	7.5	7.9
BlackRock	44.0	53.6	53.1	12.4	13.6	12.9	1.0	1.2	1.2	18.6	19.8	18.6
Calamos Asset Management	0.2	0.2	0.3	0.8	1.1	1.3	0.9	0.9	1.0	13.4	19.7	14.1
The Carlyle Group	1.3	1.8	2.2	16.6	19.3	15.8	0.7	0.9	1.1	NM	37.5	17.2
Cohen & Steers	1.6	1.8	1.8	13.9	13.9	14.6	3.3	3.6	3.6	24.2	25.5	26.4
Diamond Hill Investment Group	0.3	0.4	0.4	9.8	12.8	11.5	1.9	3.0	3.0	14.3	18.6	18.9
Eaton Vance	5.0	5.2	4.7	12.9	11.5	10.2	1.8	1.9	1.7	24.6	28.0	22.3
Federated Investors	2.5	3.0	3.2	8.4	10.8	12.2	0.7	0.8	0.9	13.2	17.8	19.7
Fortress Investment Group	1.4	2.1	1.5	8.1	5.8	3.7	2.2	3.3	2.4	23.5	14.0	9.4
Franklin Resources	32.1	36.4	34.2	10.6	10.4	9.1	3.6	4.1	3.9	16.4	17.1	15.4
GAMCO Investors	1.4	2.3	2.0	10.1	15.3	12.6	2.9	4.8	4.3	18.6	22.2	17.1
Invesco	12.8	16.1	16.0	16.2	16.3	15.9	1.6	2.0	2.0	19.4	19.9	19.0
Janus Capital Group	1.7	2.3	2.1	6.5	7.9	6.9	1.0	1.3	1.2	17.1	21.3	17.5
KKR & Co.	5.0	7.0	6.9	NA	NA	NA	4.9	6.9	6.7	8.7	13.7	9.9
Legg Mason	4.1	5.2	5.8	10.8	11.4	11.9	NA	NA	NA	NM	NM	24.9
Manning & Napier	0.2	0.2	0.2	0.3	0.4	0.4	0.4	0.5	0.4	NM	NM	NM
Oaktree Capital Management	1.5	2.3	2.5	NM	NM	NM	NA	NA	NA	13.3	9.9	9.2
Och-Ziff Capital Management Group	1.4	2.4	2.3	5.5	5.4	6.6	3.2	5.5	5.5	NM	21.3	8.5
SEI Investments Company	5.0	5.9	5.7	13.6	14.6	13.2	NA	NA	NA	24.4	21.8	20.5
T. Rowe Price	19.2	21.9	21.6	12.6	12.2	11.7	2.7	3.1	3.0	22.3	22.6	21.1
The Blackstone Group	11.0	17.8	21.8	NA	NA	NA	4.0	6.5	8.0	48.3	27.9	16.8
Virtus Investment Partners	1.5	1.8	1.6	19.9	13.8	9.8	2.5	3.1	2.7	40.0	25.9	19.4
Waddell & Reed	3.7	5.6	6.2	10.6	13.6	14.2	2.9	4.2	4.8	19.5	24.6	24.9
Westwood Holdings Group	0.4	0.5	0.5	14.1	17.0	15.2	1.9	2.7	2.7	26.9	29.8	26.8
Subgroup average	$6.7	$8.5	$8.5	10.9	11.5	10.6	2.2	3.0	3.0	22.1	22.1	18.2

(continued)

Table 30.   Asset Managers by Geography, Valuation Metrics (continued)

	Market Capitalization ($ billions)			Enterprise Value/ LTM EBITDA			Price/AUM (bps)			Price/ LTM Earnings		
	Mar/13	Dec/13	Mar/14	Mar/13	Dec/13	Mar/14	Mar/13	Dec/13	Mar/14	Mar/13	Dec/13	Mar/14
Australia												
Argo Investments Limited	$4.3	$4.2	$4.4	22.4	25.1	23.1	NA	NA	NA	24.4	26.4	24.4
Australian Foundation Investment Company	5.9	5.8	5.8	23.6	26.2	24.5	NA	NA	NA	23.6	26.5	25.2
BKI Investment Company Limited	0.7	0.7	0.8	20.3	25.4	23.0	NA	NA	NA	19.6	20.6	21.7
BT Investment Management Limited	0.8	1.3	1.7	16.6	16.1	20.4	1.3	2.1	2.7	37.1	28.9	36.7
Magellan Financial Group	1.1	1.5	2.0	NM	17.4	17.4	5.1	7.0	9.3	46.6	26.9	26.5
Milton Corporation Limited	2.4	2.4	2.5	19.5	21.6	20.7	NA	NA	NA	21.9	23.2	22.4
Platinum Investment Management Limited	3.0	3.6	4.0	14.5	18.9	16.2	13.1	15.4	17.3	23.9	30.5	25.4
Subgroup average	$2.6	$2.8	$3.0	19.5	21.5	20.8	6.5	8.2	9.8	28.2	26.1	26.0
Canada												
AGF Management Limited	$0.9	$1.1	$1.0	7.8	9.9	11.3	2.6	3.0	2.8	39.6	42.1	46.8
Brookfield Asset Management	22.8	23.9	25.1	16.1	13.3	13.4	NA	NA	NA	18.9	14.5	13.6
CI Financial	7.8	9.5	9.0	15.7	17.8	16.7	NA	NA	NA	22.7	24.9	23.2
Fiera Capital	0.6	0.9	0.9	21.3	25.7	20.2	0.7	1.1	1.1	NM	NM	57.2
Gluskin Sheff + Associates	0.5	0.7	0.8	8.3	9.8	6.6	7.2	9.6	11.5	14.0	14.8	10.9
Sprotte	0.6	0.6	0.8	10.9	26.8	NM	8.8	8.8	11.7	18.5	40.3	NM
Subgroup average	$5.5	$6.1	$6.3	13.4	17.2	13.6	4.8	5.6	6.8	22.7	27.3	30.3

(continued)

Table 30.   Asset Managers by Geography, Valuation Metrics (continued)

	Market Capitalization ($ billions)			Enterprise Value/ LTM EBITDA			Price/AUM (bps)			Price/ LTM Earnings		
	Mar/13	Dec/13	Mar/14	Mar/13	Dec/13	Mar/14	Mar/13	Dec/13	Mar/14	Mar/13	Dec/13	Mar/14
Hong Kong												
Value Partners Group	$1.1	$1.4	$1.1	NM	NM	14.6	1.4	1.7	1.3	23.5	35.3	21.5
Japan												
SPARX Group Company	$0.4	$0.6	$0.4	NM	NM	16.7	NA	NA	NA	NM	NM	32.2
United Kingdom												
Aberdeen Asset Management	$7.5	$9.5	$7.5	13.0	10.7	8.1	2.3	2.9	2.3	24.5	19.1	14.9
Alliance Trust	3.7	4.2	4.3	7.6	4.9	5.0	NA	NA	NA	9.9	5.8	5.6
Ashmore Group	3.6	4.5	3.7	8.3	9.0	7.5	7.8	9.8	8.2	13.5	14.0	13.7
Caledonia Investments	1.6	1.7	1.8	9.4	5.5	5.6	NA	NA	NA	10.0	6.2	6.3
Henderson Group	2.5	4.0	4.7	10.2	13.3	15.1	4.0	6.2	7.4	17.3	21.7	28.0
Jupiter Fund Management	2.0	2.8	3.2	10.0	11.1	11.8	6.2	8.8	10.2	23.1	20.5	20.0
RIT Capital Partners	2.9	3.2	3.5	NM	NA	6.6	NA	NA	NA	NM	15.4	6.1
Schroders	8.4	11.2	11.3	5.2	8.6	6.6	3.2	4.3	4.3	20.8	22.8	20.6
Subgroup average	$4.0	$5.1	$5.0	9.1	9.0	8.3	4.7	6.4	6.5	17.0	15.7	14.4
Switzerland												
GAM Holding	$2.8	$3.2	$2.9	9.5	8.4	7.8	2.4	2.8	2.6	31.7	17.3	13.4
Partners Group Holding	6.3	6.9	7.2	21.1	22.7	22.4	16.2	17.7	18.7	23.6	21.3	20.7
Subgroup average	$4.6	$5.1	$5.1	15.3	15.6	15.1	9.3	10.3	10.7	27.7	19.3	17.1
South Africa												
Coronation Fund Managers Limited	$1.8	$2.7	$3.3	16.5	13.9	17.3	0.4	0.5	0.7	24.3	19.2	23.8

(continued)

Table 30. Asset Managers by Geography, Valuation Metrics (continued)

	Market Capitalization ($ billions)			Enterprise Value/ LTM EBITDA			Price/AUM (bps)			Price/ LTM Earnings		
	Mar/13	Dec/13	Mar/14	Mar/13	Dec/13	Mar/14	Mar/13	Dec/13	Mar/14	Mar/13	Dec/13	Mar/14
Singapore												
ARA Asset Management Limited	$1.2	$1.2	$1.2	15.5	17.8	16.1	NA	NA	NA	22.3	22.5	21.0
CitySpring Infrastructure Trust	0.6	0.6	0.6	12.4	13.4	14.3	NA	NA	NA	38.6	NM	NM
Subgroup average	$0.9	$0.9	$0.9	14.0	15.6	15.2	NA	NA	NA	NA	NA	NA
South America												
Tarpon Investimentos	$0.3	$0.3	$0.3	12.0	12.0	6.6	NA	NA	NA	20.3	17.5	9.8
Average	$5.0	$6.1	$6.1	12.5	13.7	12.5	3.4	4.4	4.6	23.0	22.1	20.1
Median	$2.4	$2.8	$3.2	12.4	13.5	12.8	2.5	3.1	2.9	22.1	21.3	19.9

Notes: All dates are as of end of month. LTM = last 12 months. NM = not meaningful. NA = not available.

MAJOR RISKS

CAPITAL MARKETS

The fluctuations in global fixed-income and equity markets serve as a constant influence on asset manager earnings. Although financial markets have generally trended higher over multidecade periods, severe market dislocations can have a dramatic impact on the ability of an asset manager to generate sufficient revenue to cover its costs. To smooth revenue volatility, publicly traded asset managers tend to strive for (1) a balance of equities and fixed income in their product offerings and (2) a broad geographical base of clients and capital market exposures.

With regard to PE managers, adverse capital market conditions can have an especially acute impact on buyout funds as the ability to raise financing (primarily in the high-yield bond and bank loan markets) diminishes and the time to exit via IPO is reduced.

INVESTMENT PERFORMANCE

Managers offering actively managed investment strategies are subject to the risk of underperforming (1) predetermined investment benchmarks and (2) peers offering similarly managed strategies. Underperformance is routinely measured in pure absolute terms but is increasingly looked at in risk-adjusted terms as well (return per unit of risk, derived from either the Sharpe or information ratio).

Analysts should focus closely on the performance of a firm's largest "flagship" offerings and be aware of the skew these products can introduce in firmwide asset-weighted performance metrics. It is not uncommon for an asset manager to rely heavily on one to three mainstay products to generate a significant portion of its revenue. Analysts should also examine performance at the individual product level to determine the breadth of outperformance and a manager's ability to offer a full range of attractive strategies across investment disciplines.

Table 31 presents data from Janus Capital Group's 2013 annual report, providing an aggregate view of the firm's investment performance versus its peers (Morningstar quartiles) and benchmarks.

Table 31. Investment Performance Summary: Period Ending 31 December 2013

	1 Year	3 Year	5 Year
Percentage of assets in top two Morningstar quartiles			
Complex-wide mutual fund assets	46%	46%	53%
Fundamental equity mutual fund assets	38	39	54
Fixed-income mutual fund assets	100	100	53
Percentage of strategies that outperformed respective benchmarks			
Mathematical equity strategies	59%	79%	42%
Percentage of complex-wide mutual funds with four- or five-star overall Morningstar rating			
Complex-wide mutual funds		56%	

Source: Janus Capital Group, "Annual Report 2013" (http://ir.janus.com/docs.aspx?iid=4050265).

OPERATIONAL RISK

Technology has served as a key factor in connecting and driving efficiencies within and across global financial markets. Asset managers rely on technology to conduct research, run automated trading platforms, construct portfolios, account for portfolio securities, model risk, compute performance, allocate trades across accounts, and perform other key activities. Any system disruptions or failures represent the potential for serious reputational and regulatory risk. To mitigate such risk, asset managers often rely on large internal operational and technology teams or on third-party specialist vendors. In addition, many asset managers attempt to reduce technology-related risk by building elaborate disaster recovery plans and redundant systems.

HUMAN CAPITAL/KEY MAN RISK

Portfolio managers or other key investment personnel who serve as the public face of a successful investment strategy can often take on celebrity status among the investing public. The loss of key investment personnel who are perceived as critical components of a successful investment strategy can lead to accelerated and significant withdrawals of client assets, with a resulting reduction in asset management revenues. Following the departure of chief investment officer David Iben from Tradewinds Global Investors (a Nuveen Investments affiliate), the firm's AUM declined from $38 billion to $10.3 billion in a matter of 10 months.[55]

Equity incentives and deferred compensation packages are most often used to attract and retain key investment professionals. Moreover, the use of portfolio management teams, with multiple portfolio managers being named on a single portfolio, often serves to mitigate the risk of a departure.

COUNTERPARTY RISK

Asset management firms interact with a number of counterparties (e.g., brokerages, prime brokerages, custodians) to trade and settle securities and derivatives contracts. Understanding the risks that counterparties pose, especially in the wake of the 2008 financial crisis, is a critical function involving the successful coordination of a multitude of internal departments. Typically, asset managers monitor counterparties based on a number of factors, including creditworthiness, trading capacity, concentration exposure, and regulatory oversight. These factors, among others, are monitored continuously in the measuring and selecting of counterparties.

Although asset managers clearly face a number of key risks, the 2008 financial crisis spawned questions from regulators about the risks posed by asset managers themselves to the financial markets. An asset manager's clients are the legal owners of the assets held in SMAs, and CIV investors own an undivided share of the underlying assets of a fund. Accordingly, asset managers are typically acting in an agency role and thus have largely escaped the new regulations imposed on other financial institutions, such as banks. According to Andrew Haldane, executive director for financial stability at the Bank of England, "As an agency function, asset managers do not bear credit, market and liquidity risk on their portfolios.... Fluctuations in asset values do not threaten the insolvency of an asset manager as they would a bank. Asset managers are, to a large extent, insolvency-remote."[56]

---

[55]Randy Diamond, "Tradewinds' AUM Falls 72% in 10 Months," *Pensions & Investments* (24 December 2012): www.pionline.com/article/20121224/PRINT/312249988/tradewinds-aum-falls-72-in-10-months.

[56]Andrew G. Haldane, "The Age of Asset Management?" Speech given at London Business School (4 April 2014): www.bankofengland.co.uk/publications/Documents/speeches/2014/speech723.pdf.

APPENDIX A. DATA

Table A1. **Total Net Assets, Number of Funds, Number of Share Classes, and Number of Shareholder Accounts of the Mutual Fund Industry**
(as of year-end)

Year	Total Net Assets ($ billions)	Number of Funds	Number of Share Classes	Number of Shareholder Accounts[a] (thousands)
1940	$0.45	68	—	296
1945	1.28	73	—	498
1950	2.53	98	—	939
1955	7.84	125	—	2,085
1960	17.03	161	—	4,898
1965	35.22	170	—	6,709
1970	47.62	361	—	10,690
1975	45.87	426	—	9,876
1976	51.28	452	—	9,060
1977	48.94	477	—	8,693
1978	55.84	505	—	8,658
1979	94.51	526	—	9,790
1980	134.76	564	—	12,088
1981	241.37	665	—	17,499
1982	296.68	857	—	21,448
1983	292.99	1,026	—	24,605
1984	370.68	1,243	1,243	27,636
1985	495.39	1,528	1,528	34,098
1986	715.67	1,835	1,835	45,374
1987	769.17	2,312	2,312	53,717
1988	809.37	2,737	2,737	54,056
1989	980.67	2,935	2,935	57,560
1990	1,065.19	3,079	3,177	61,948

(continued)

Table A1. **Total Net Assets, Number of Funds, Number of Share Classes, and Number of Shareholder Accounts of the Mutual Fund Industry**
(as of year-end) (continued)

Year	Total Net Assets ($ billions)	Number of Funds	Number of Share Classes	Number of Shareholder Accounts[a] (thousands)
1991	$1,393.19	3,403	3,587	68,332
1992	1,642.54	3,824	4,208	79,931
1993	2,069.96	4,534	5,562	94,015
1994	2,155.32	5,325	7,697	114,383
1995	2,811.29	5,725	9,007	131,219
1996	3,525.80	6,248	10,352	149,933
1997	4,468.20	6,684	12,002	170,299
1998	5,525.21	7,314	13,720	194,029
1999	6,846.34	7,791	15,262	226,212
2000	6,964.63	8,155	16,738	244,705
2001	6,974.91	8,305	18,022	248,701
2002	6,383.48	8,243	18,983	251,123
2003	7,402.42	8,125	19,317	260,698
2004	8,095.45	8,042	20,035	269,468
2005	8,891.11	7,974	20,548	275,479
2006	10,397.88	8,117	21,249	288,594
2007	11,999.73	8,023	21,610	292,553
2008	9,602.57	8,019	22,232	264,597
2009	11,112.67	7,659	21,661	269,449
2010	11,831.33	7,548	21,907	291,299
2011	11,626.49	7,580	22,249	272,628
2012	13,043.67	7,582	22,605	257,074
2013	15,017.68	7,707	23,353	264,848

Notes: Data tables are from Investment Company Institute, *2014 Investment Company Fact Book*. Data for funds that invest primarily in other mutual funds were excluded from the series.
[a]Number of shareholder accounts includes a mix of individual and omnibus accounts.

Table A2. Total Net Assets of the Mutual Fund Industry by Composite Investment Objective
($ billions, as of year-end)

Year	Equity Funds			Hybrid Funds	Bond Funds							Money Market Funds	
	Capital Appreciation	World	Total Return		Investment Grade	High Yield	World	Government	Multisector	State Municipal	National Municipal	Taxable	Tax Exempt
2000	$1,433.95	$564.75	$1,936.21	$360.92	$245.69	$109.94	$29.61	$124.87	$35.04	$131.92	$146.49	$1,611.38	$233.87
2001	1,105.24	444.47	1,843.26	358.03	311.29	109.20	28.05	154.14	39.70	139.78	156.44	2,026.23	259.08
2002	765.54	369.37	1,508.38	335.28	406.26	108.11	29.72	218.98	46.64	152.72	177.41	1,988.78	276.30
2003	1,041.14	535.05	2,078.67	447.55	473.95	158.99	38.19	197.99	54.57	149.26	187.05	1,749.73	290.29
2004	1,148.56	716.20	2,479.30	552.01	518.25	167.44	47.41	176.61	59.73	144.09	184.15	1,589.70	312.00
2005	1,232.82	955.73	2,698.11	621.34	570.10	158.48	56.62	167.34	64.81	147.46	191.50	1,690.45	336.37
2006	1,319.36	1,360.45	3,153.76	731.36	640.32	174.40	78.13	153.15	83.41	154.42	210.67	1,969.42	369.03
2007	1,419.59	1,718.57	3,275.73	821.28	760.36	174.75	107.43	158.19	103.93	155.94	218.21	2,617.67	468.09
2008	808.68	898.60	1,930.43	562.05	736.42	117.59	103.80	188.04	86.93	135.09	202.70	3,338.56	493.68
2009	1,085.71	1,307.98	2,479.23	717.78	1,050.05	197.09	146.42	210.31	143.72	159.26	299.24	2,916.96	398.94
2010	1,248.18	1,540.98	2,807.67	842.04	1,241.30	241.88	214.10	225.40	192.31	156.16	317.38	2,473.92	330.01
2011	1,178.82	1,355.34	2,679.63	882.98	1,364.79	267.25	256.01	241.94	211.40	158.89	338.01	2,399.72	291.70
2012	1,319.91	1,611.59	3,008.59	1,030.82	1,571.62	335.70	320.56	297.98	274.52	177.53	401.32	2,406.10	287.43
2013	1,725.21	2,034.17	4,004.48	1,270.20	1,450.83	411.52	338.99	239.05	326.70	144.82	353.37	2,447.72	270.61

Note: Data for funds that invest primarily in other mutual funds were excluded from the series.

Table A3. Net New Cash Flow[a] of Long-Term Mutual Funds
($ millions)

Year	Total	Equity Funds	Hybrid Funds	Bond Funds
1984	$19,194	$4,336	$1,801	$13,058
1985	73,490	6,643	3,720	63,127
1986	129,991	20,386	6,988	102,618
1987	29,776	19,231	3,748	6,797
1988	−23,119	−14,948	−3,684	−4,488
1989	8,731	6,774	3,183	−1,226
1990	21,211	12,915	1,483	6,813
1991	106,213	39,888	7,089	59,236
1992	171,696	78,983	21,833	70,881
1993	242,049	127,261	44,229	70,559
1994	75,160	114,525	23,105	−62,470
1995	122,208	124,392	3,899	−6,082
1996	231,874	216,937	12,177	2,760
1997	272,030	227,107	16,499	28,424
1998	241,796	156,875	10,311	74,610
1999	169,780	187,565	−13,705	−4,080
2000	228,874	315,742	−36,722	−50,146
2001	129,188	33,633	7,285	88,269
2002	120,583	−29,048	8,043	141,587
2003	215,843	144,416	39,066	32,360
2004	209,851	171,831	53,082	−15,062
2005	192,086	123,718	42,841	25,527
2006	227,103	147,548	19,870	59,685
2007	224,254	73,035	40,330	110,889
2008	−224,997	−229,576	−25,652	30,232
2009	389,155	−2,019	19,888	371,285
2010	241,271	−24,477	35,256	230,492
2011	25,846	−129,024	39,763	115,107
2012	195,922	−152,234	46,531	301,624
2013	151,835	159,784	72,514	−80,463

Notes: Data for funds that invest primarily in other mutual funds were excluded from the series. Components many not add to the total because of rounding.

[a]Net new cash flow is the dollar value of new sales minus redemptions combined with net exchanges.

Table A4. Worldwide Total Net Assets of Mutual Funds
($ millions, as of year-end)

	2008	2009	2010	2011	2012	2013
World	$18,918,982	$22,945,327	$24,709,854	$23,795,808	$26,835,850	$30,049,934
Americas	$10,580,914	$12,578,297	$13,597,527	$13,529,258	$15,138,443	$17,156,409
Argentina	3,867	4,470	5,179	6,808	9,185	11,179
Brazil	479,321	783,970	980,448	1,008,928	1,070,998	1,018,641
Canada	416,031	565,156	636,947	753,606	856,504	940,580
Chile	17,587	34,227	38,243	33,425	37,900	39,291
Costa Rica	1,098	1,309	1,470	1,266	1,484	1,933
Mexico	60,435	70,659	98,094	92,743	112,201	120,518
Trinidad and Tobago	N/A	5,832	5,812	5,989	6,505	6,586
United States	9,602,574	11,112,674	11,831,334	11,626,493	13,043,666	15,017,682
Europe	$6,231,115	$7,545,535	$7,903,389	$7,220,298	$8,230,059	$9,374,830
Austria	93,269	99,628	94,670	81,038	89,125	90,633
Belgium	105,057	106,721	96,288	81,505	81,651	91,528
Bulgaria	226	256	302	291	324	504
Czech Republic	5,260	5,436	5,508	4,445	5,001	5,131
Denmark	65,182	83,024	89,800	84,891	103,506	118,702
Finland	48,750	66,131	71,210	62,193	73,985	88,462
France	1,591,082	1,805,641	1,617,176	1,382,068	1,473,085	1,531,500
Germany	237,986	317,543	333,713	293,011	327,640	382,976
Greece	12,189	12,434	8,627	5,213	6,011	6,742
Hungary	9,188	11,052	11,532	7,193	8,570	12,158
Ireland	720,486	860,515	1,014,104	1,061,051	1,276,601	1,439,867
Italy	263,588	279,474	234,313	180,754	181,720	215,553
Liechtenstein	20,489	30,329	35,387	32,606	31,951	36,235
Luxembourg	1,860,763	2,293,973	2,512,874	2,277,465	2,641,964	3,030,665
Malta	N/A	N/A	N/A	2,132	3,033	3,160
Netherlands	77,379	95,512	85,924	69,156	76,145	85,304
Norway	41,157	71,170	84,505	79,999	98,723	109,325
Poland	17,782	23,025	25,595	18,463	25,883	27,858
Portugal	13,572	15,808	11,004	7,321	7,509	9,625

(continued)

Table A4. Worldwide Total Net Assets of Mutual Funds
($ millions, as of year-end) (continued)

	2008	2009	2010	2011	2012	2013
Romania	326	1,134	1,713	2,388	2,613	4,000
Russia	2,026	3,182	3,917	3,072	N/A	N/A
Slovakia	3,841	4,222	4,349	3,191	2,951	3,292
Slovenia	2,067	2,610	2,663	2,279	2,370	2,506
Spain	270,983	269,611	216,915	195,220	191,284	248,234
Sweden	113,331	170,277	205,449	179,707	205,733	252,878
Switzerland	135,052	168,260	261,893	273,061	310,686	397,080
Turkey	15,404	19,426	19,545	14,048	16,478	14,078
United Kingdom	504,681	729,141	854,413	816,537	985,517	1,166,834
Asia Pacific	$2,037,536	$2,715,234	$3,067,323	$2,921,276	$3,322,198	$3,375,828
Australia	841,133	1,198,838	1,455,850	1,440,128	1,667,128	1,624,081
China	276,303	381,207	364,985	339,037	437,449	479,957
Hong Kong	N/A	N/A	N/A	N/A	N/A	N/A
India	62,805	130,284	111,421	87,519	114,489	107,895
Japan	575,327	660,666	785,504	745,383	738,488	774,126
South Korea	221,992	264,573	266,495	226,716	267,582	285,173
New Zealand	10,612	17,657	19,562	23,709	31,145	34,185
Pakistan	1,985	2,224	2,290	2,984	3,159	3,464
Philippines	1,263	1,488	2,184	2,363	3,566	4,662
Taiwan	46,116	58,297	59,032	53,437	59,192	62,286
Africa	$69,417	$106,261	$141,615	$124,976	$145,150	$142,868
South Africa	69,417	106,261	141,615	124,976	145,150	142,868

Notes: N/A = not available. Funds of funds are not included except for France, Italy, and Luxembourg. Data include home-domiciled funds, except for Hong Kong, South Korea, and New Zealand, which include home- and foreign-domiciled funds. Components may not add to the total because of rounding.

Table A5. Exchange-Traded Funds: Total Net Assets by Type of Fund
($ millions, as of year-end)

		Investment Objective						Legal Status			Memo
		Equity							1940 Act ETFs		
		Domestic Equity									
Year	Total	Broad Based	Sector[a]	Global/ International	Commodities[b]	Hybrid	Bond	Hybrid	Bond	Non-1940 Act ETFs[c]	Funds of Funds[d]
1993	$464	$464	—	—	—	—	—	$464	—	—	—
1994	424	424	—	—	—	—	—	424	—	—	—
1995	1,052	1,052	—	—	—	—	—	1,052	—	—	—
1996	2,411	2,159	—	$252	—	—	—	2,411	—	—	—
1997	6,707	6,200	—	506	—	—	—	6,707	—	—	—
1998	15,568	14,058	$484	1,026	—	—	—	15,568	—	—	—
1999	33,873	29,374	2,507	1,992	—	—	—	33,873	—	—	—
2000	65,585	60,529	3,015	2,041	—	—	—	65,585	—	—	—
2001	82,993	74,752	5,224	3,016	—	—	—	82,993	—	—	—
2002	102,143	86,985	5,919	5,324	—	—	$3,915	102,143	—	—	—
2003	150,983	120,430	11,901	13,984	—	—	4,667	150,983	—	—	—
2004	227,540	163,730	20,315	33,644	$1,335	—	8,516	226,205	—	$1,335	—
2005	300,820	186,832	28,975	65,210	4,798	—	15,004	296,022	—	4,798	—
2006	422,550	232,487	43,655	111,194	14,699	—	20,514	407,850	—	14,699	—
2007	608,422	300,930	64,117	179,702	28,906	$119	34,648	579,517	—	28,906	—
2008	531,288	266,161	58,374	113,684	35,728	132	57,209	495,314	$245	35,728	$97
2009	777,128	304,044	82,053	209,315	74,528	169	107,018	701,586	1,014	74,528	824
2010	991,989	372,377	103,807	276,622	101,081	322	137,781	888,198	2,736	101,055	1,294
2011	1,048,134	400,696	108,548	245,114	109,176	377	184,222	934,216	5,049	108,868	1,580
2012	1,337,112	509,338	135,378	328,521	120,019	656	243,203	1,206,974	10,257	119,881	2,227
2013	1,674,616	761,701	202,706	398,834	64,044	1,469	245,862	1,596,691	14,055	63,869	2,659

Note: Components may not add to the total because of rounding.
[a]This category includes funds both registered and not registered under the Investment Company Act of 1940.
[b]This category includes funds—both registered and not registered under the Investment Company Act of 1940—that invest primarily in commodities, currencies, and futures.
[c]The funds in this category are not registered under the Investment Company Act of 1940.
[d]Data for ETFs that invest primarily in other ETFs were excluded from the totals.

Table A6. Exchange-Traded Funds: Net Issuance by Type of Fund
($ millions)

		Investment Objective						Legal Status			Memo
		Equity						1940 Act ETFs		Non-1940 Act ETFs[c]	Funds of Funds[d]
		Domestic Equity									
Year	Total	Broad Based	Sector[a]	Global/ International	Commodities[b]	Hybrid	Bond	Index	Actively Managed		
1993	$442	$442	—	—	—	—	—	$442	—	—	—
1994	−28	−28	—	—	—	—	—	−28	—	—	—
1995	443	443	—	—	—	—	—	443	—	—	—
1996	1,108	842	—	$266	—	—	—	1,108	—	—	—
1997	3,466	3,160	—	306	—	—	—	3,466	—	—	—
1998	6,195	5,158	$484	553	—	—	—	6,195	—	—	—
1999	11,929	10,221	1,596	112	—	—	—	11,929	—	—	—
2000	42,508	40,591	1,033	884	—	—	—	42,508	—	—	—
2001	31,012	26,911	2,735	1,366	—	—	—	31,012	—	—	—
2002	45,302	35,477	2,304	3,792	—	—	$3,729	45,302	—	—	—
2003	15,810	5,737	3,587	5,764	—	—	721	15,810	—	—	—
2004	56,375	29,084	6,514	15,645	$1,353	—	3,778	55,021	—	$1,353	—
2005	56,729	16,941	6,719	23,455	2,859	—	6,756	53,871	—	2,859	—
2006	73,995	21,589	9,780	28,423	8,475	—	5,729	65,520	—	8,475	—
2007	150,617	61,152	18,122	48,842	9,062	$122	13,318	141,555	—	9,062	—
2008	177,220	88,105	30,296	25,243	10,567	58	22,952	166,372	$281	10,567	$107
2009	116,469	−11,842	14,329	39,599	28,410	15	45,958	87,336	724	28,410	237
2010	117,982	28,317	10,187	41,527	8,155	144	29,652	108,141	1,711	8,129	433
2011	117,642	34,653	9,682	24,250	2,940	72	46,045	112,437	2,567	2,639	389
2012	185,394	57,739	14,307	51,896	8,892	246	52,318	171,329	5,025	9,041	510
2013	179,885	99,470	34,434	62,807	−29,870	849	12,195	205,323	4,468	−29,906	1,180

Note: Components may not add to the total because of rounding.

[a]This category includes funds both registered and not registered under the Investment Company Act of 1940.

[b]This category includes funds—both registered and not registered under the Investment Company Act of 1940—that invest primarily in commodities, currencies, and futures.

[c]The funds in this category are not registered under the Investment Company Act of 1940.

[d]Data for ETFs that invest primarily in other ETFs were excluded from the totals.

INDUSTRY RESOURCES

REGULATORY AGENCIES

Commission de Surveillance du Secteur Financier (Luxembourg)
www.cssf.lu/en

European Commission, UCITS
http://ec.europa.eu/internal_market/investment/index_en.htm

Financial Stability Oversight Council: Established under the Dodd–Frank Wall Street Reform and Consumer Protection Act to provide broad oversight of the US financial system
www.treasury.gov/initiatives/fsoc/pages/home.aspx

Financial Industry Regulatory Authority (FINRA)
1735 K Street Northwest
Washington, DC 20006
FINRA Call Center: +1 (301) 590-6500
www.finra.org

Securities and Exchange Commission (United States)
100 F Street Northeast
Washington, DC 20549
+1 (202) 942-8088
www.sec.gov

> **Mutual Fund Search**
> www.sec.gov/edgar/searchedgar/mutualsearch.htm
>
> **Division of Investment Management**
> www.sec.gov/investment#.U53Q7_ldWSo
>
> **Investment Adviser Search**
> www.adviserinfo.sec.gov/IAPD/Content/Search/iapd_Search.aspx

US Commodity Futures Trading Commission
Three Lafayette Centre
1155 21st Street Northwest
Washington, DC 20581
+1 (202) 418-5000
www.cftc.gov

ASSET MANAGEMENT INDUSTRY

Casey Quirk: Dedicated asset management business strategy and research consultant
www.caseyquirk.com

Cerulli Associates: Global asset management data aggregator and researcher
www.cerulli.com

European Fund and Asset Management Association (EFAMA):
European investment industry association
www.efama.org

FUSE Research Network: Asset management researcher and consultant focused on the US retail market
www.fuse-research.com

Greenwich Associates: Financial services research and consulting firm with deep institutional asset management expertise
www.greenwich.com

Heidrick & Struggles: Asset management recruiting firm; industry compensation surveys
www.heidrick.com

International Investment Funds Association (IIFA)
www.iifa.ca

Investment Company Institute (ICI): Retail industry trade group; conducts comprehensive US investment industry research; excellent data source
www.ici.org

McLagan: Industry compensation benchmarking and metrics
www.mclagan.com/asset_management

Sheffield Haworth: Global executive search; industry research
www.sheffieldhaworth.com

Strategic Insight: Research and data provider focused on the retail industry
www.sionline.com

ASSET MANAGEMENT INDUSTRY NEWS

Citywire: Global mutual fund news and performance
http://citywireglobal.com

FundFire: Institutional asset management news and information
www.fundfire.com

Ignites: Retail asset management news
www.ignites.com

InvestmentWires: Retail- and retirement-related news
http://investmentwires.com

InvestmentNews: News and analysis relevant to US financial advisers
www.investmentnews.com

CLOSED-END FUNDS

Closed-End Fund Association
www.cefa.com

EXCHANGE-TRADED FUNDS

ETF.com: ETF-dedicated news, research, and data
www.ETF.com

ETFGI: Global ETF industry research
www.etfgi.com

ICI Exchange-Traded Funds Resource Center
www.ici.org/etf_resources

Morningstar: Performance and investment research data
www.morningstar.com

INVESTMENT PRODUCT–SPECIFIC NEWS

Pensions & Investments: Institutional asset management news, research, and analysis
www.pionline.com

Institutional Investor: Global institutional coverage
www.institutionalinvestor.com

ALTERNATIVE INVESTMENTS

BarclayHedge: Alternative investment industry research, rankings, indexes
www.barclayhedge.com

Greenwich Roundtable: Industry think tank dedicated to alternatives
www.greenwichroundtable.org

Hedge Fund Research (HFR): Industry data and indexes
www.hedgefundresearch.com

PE HUB: Global private equity news
www.pehub.com

Preqin: Data and research on alternatives
www.preqin.com

Venture Capital Journal: Venture capital news and data
http://privatemarkets.thomsonreuters.com/venture-capital-journal

Index Investing

William F. Sharpe, "Indexed Investing: A Prosaic Way to Beat the Average Investor," presentation at the Monterey Institute of International Studies (1 May 2002): http://web.stanford.edu/~wfsharpe/art/talks/indexed_investing.htm. Sharpe, professor emeritus of finance at Stanford University, makes the classic indexing argument.

INVESTMENT DATA AND STRATEGY ATTRIBUTION

Bloomberg: Global data, analysis, news; investment performance databases
www.bloomberg.com

eVestment: Institutional separately managed account database
www.evestment.com

FactSet: Holdings-based returns analysis
www.factset.com

PSN: Institutional separately managed account database
www.informais.com/psnenterprise.html

S&P Capital IQ: Global data; financial analytics
www.capitaliq.com

Zephyr: Returns-based investment software
www.styleadvisor.com

SPECIALIST INVESTMENT BANKS

Berkshire Capital
www.berkcap.com/Home.aspx

Cambridge International Partners
www.cambintl.com

Colchester Partners
www.colchesterpartners.com

Freeman & Co.
www.freeman-co.com

Grail Partners
www.grailpartners.com

Made in the USA
San Bernardino, CA
25 October 2016